DRACULA'S DAUGHTER:

AND OTHER STORIES

BY

MARTIN HUBNER

COPYRIGHT: C. MARTIN HUBNER

WWW.RAINTREEPRODUCTIONSLTD.CO.UK
London/Dec.2014. All Rights Reserved.

FOR JANE:
THANKS FOR ALL THE HELP, AND WITH LOVE.

CONTENTS

Dracula's Daughter
Lawn Mower
Chris Somebody
Foreign Places
La Dona Suena
In Secundis
Over The Top
Antiques
Not In My Back Yard
Violence

Democracy
In Excelis Gloria
Summer Exhibition
Twelve Gardens

DRACULA'S DAUGHTER

Vampire:

1734. Magyar *vampire*- identical form in Slav langs.; the ult. origin maybe Turk, *uber* witch.

1. A preternatural being of malignant nature (in the orig. and usual form of the belief, a reanimated corpse), supposed to seek nourishment, or do harm, by sucking the blood of sleeping persons; a man or woman endowed with similar habits.

2. *transf.* A person of a malignant and loathsome character, esp. one who preys ruthlessly on others; a vile and cruel extractor or extortioner 1741.

Shorter Oxford Dictionary (Third Edition 1973.)

The vampire is said to be the restless undead. There are many types of vampires in beliefs found all over the world. A vampire is either living dead – a resurrected corpse – or the ghost of a corpse that leaves its grave at night and walks the world of the living dead to feed off them to survive. Some vampires, particularly in Eastern, Middle Eastern and tribal mythologies, are demons that attack at night, and are associated with night terrors.

*Western fiction and film have popularized the vampire as an entirely different creature, a glamorous and seductive living dead person who bites people
(usually on the neck) to drink their blood.*

The Encyclopedia of Ghosts and Spirits by Rosemary Ellen Guiley (Third Edition 2007)

Every so often one gets frightened by what seems to be an incredible coincidence or is it just that certain things happen that way, and appear to be like a coincidence. Often when this happens some people feel a little nervous, & need to tell someone about it. A few people think it is to do with the supernatural & possibly darker spirits.

Jonathan Cunliffe, was an out of work film director who did up small flats in North London, when there appeared to be no film work on the horizon, which was quite often. On one of those days, on an early June morning, Jonathan was wheeling through a few property websites when he spotted a small studio flat for sale in Belsize Park, just off Haverstock Hill, a comfortable middle class suburb.

'Always a safe bet, location, location and all that......' he mumbled to himself.

Jonathan emailed the estate agent, called Abdul, in his Camden Town office, and arranged to meet him outside the block of flats to view this property at 11am that morning.

Abdul turned up fifteen minutes late apologizing about the traffic, handing Jonathan details of the flat. He told Jonathan that the flat was on the third floor and had actually been re-possessed. They went up in the lift and walked down a long corridor to the flat. When they arrived Jonathan noticed that attached to the front door was a heavy metal bar over a huge thick steel door with a big padlock on. There was a re-possession notice on the door too.

'What's going on here, looks like Fort Knox?' said Jonathan

'Well, there has been a bit of trouble...' Abdul stated.

'Looks like they are trying to keep someone out,' Jonathan said.

'Well all I have heard is that there has been a tall dark haired woman wondering up and down the corridors, banging on doors and screeching,' Abdul revealed.

'Not the best way to sell a flat! Can we go in now?' Jonathan asked.

'Seems that she may have been the owner who was repossessed,' Abdul replied.

'Not my problem,' retorted Jonathan, thinking that there might be a deal to be done here.

Abdul then fumbles through a set of keys, tries all the keys, but cannot gain entrance. He then makes a mobile phone call and finds out that the locks have been changed again, hence his inability to get in.

They take the lift down together in silence, with Jonathan reading over the flat details. They go through the main entrance to the flats.

Jonathan tries to stay calm, although he is annoyed, and asks Abdul when he can actually see inside the flat, and if any sort of offer on it has already been made. Abdul says he will have to get back to Jonathan later in the day.

Abdul then scurries off, leaving Jonathan on the pavement looking up at the block of flats.

'Bloody waste of time, bloody estate agents don't know what they are doing…,' Jonathan mumbled to himself…

Jonathan then walks down the street, and looks into the window of another estate agent on the corner, opposite Belsize tube station. He notices another studio flat for sale in the same block and wonders whether it is the same one, thinking that maybe they have got the proper set of keys. If they had, he could now have a look at the flat.

Jonathan goes into the office, and goes up to the desk of an estate agent called Michael whom he knows from past enquiries and a flat sale he did a few years before.

'Morning Michael, I see you have got a studio flat for sale in that block down the road,' asked Jonathan.

'Yes we have, nice little property, but probably needs some work doing to it,' Michael replied.

'It is not the one on the third floor where there has been some trouble. Some sort of re-possession ?' Jonathan asked probingly.

'No, not that one. Apparently some woman all dressed in black, and with dense black hair has been causing trouble, screaming and banging on doors, saying that they have stolen her flat from her,' Michael said quickly.

'Really, sounds like some sort of vampire movie,' Jonathan retorted.

'I wouldn't touch it with a barge pole, there seems to be lots of problems associated with that flat,' Michael cut in.

'Maybe it is owned by Dracula's daughter who forgot to pay her mortgage,' Jonathan quips.

Michael then shows Jonathan computer details of a similar flat on the ground floor of the block, and suggests that this might be a better deal given that they are at similar prices.

Jonathan steps out of the office to make a phone call to one of his mates who works in the film business as a casting director, called Jack Fontaine.

They discuss where they should have lunch in Soho, in central London, and at what time. They are going to discuss a film script.

For some time now Jack has been saying to Jonathan that if he wants to make another movie he ought to look at lower budget Horror films with budgets of up to USD $1 million which are getting made. To date Jonathan had worked on higher budget films. But given the economic uncertainty after the near global melt-down in 2008-2009, he was finding it very difficult to raise money for films even though he told everyone that these days a well-produced film was a safer bet than your average high street bank.

So the idea was to discuss a possible horror film script over their lunch.

Jonathan then goes back into the estate agent offices and asks Michael when he could see this other studio flat. A 12.30 pm meeting is set up outside the block of flats again.

Jonathan goes for an expresso coffee and gets to the block of flats just before 12.30. His Blackberry phone rings, he sees it is Jack Fontaine calling.

'Jack, so soon, you could wait till our lunch ?' asked Jonathan.

'I am afraid the director I am working with on this Hungarian feature film wants a meeting today. Just turned up out of the blue, meant to be arriving next week. Can we postpone this lunch?' suggested Jack.

'Sure I am not doing anything, just looking at studio flats in a block off Haverstock Hill in Belsize Park, my other job…you know,' Jonathan cuts in.

'What the one with the big steel door with the metal bar across?' asked Jack

'Jesus Jack how the hell did you know I was looking at that flat?' Jonathan shouted out somewhat taken aback.

'Was it a tall dark haired lady dressed in black, causing trouble outside the flats? The police were called by the caretaker to the flat,' Jack stated.

'Shit a brick, Jack how do you know all this, sounds very spooky and weird. Might have our horror film script here. When I come to think of it the third floor corridor had an oppressive feeling, a kind of dullness. Do you know this dark haired vampire bitch then Jack?' Jonathan asked

'Sure, she is a Greek actress she has told me all about her flat and how she thinks she was illegally re-possessed, very bitter women, wants revenge,' retorted Jack.

'Any good as an actress? She could take the lead. We could do a re-make of that French erotic horror film made by Jesus Franco. What was it called? You remember? Oh yea, 'Female Vampire' made years ago in the mid 1970's,' Jonathan said.

'Isn't that the one where a mute woman needs sex like a vampire needs blood, in order to stay alive forever. She sucks the life out of her male and female victims while performing oral sex on them,' Jacks replied.

'You remember all the best bits Jack. But has this Greek actress lost her marbles or what?' enquired Jonathan.

'Well she keeps coming around the office and just sits there. She is very sad and then gets very angry, and then disappears for a week or two,' Jack said.

'Have you used her in any films Jack?' asked Jonathan

'A while back, in that biblical series shot in North Africa,' stated Jack.

'A kind of Irene Papas actress?' Jonathan asked

'Yes that sort of thing. Listen I better go, call me next week and we will re-arrange that lunch. Work on your treatment for this horror film.
I have got guys who will put the money up for a good gory commercial horror script,' Jack said enthusiastically.

'What no pre-sales to North America or film guarantees or film completion bonds? 'Jonathan asked.

'Nope, just soft money with not too many strings attached, provided it can be shot for a million bucks or less. Got to go. Ciao,' Jack said rather quickly.

'Soft money indeed....' Jonathan said to himself.

After a protracted negotiation period, Jonathan bought the third floor flat in that block, in Belsize Park. He had the metal door removed, after it was confirmed to him that the dark haired lady in black had been barred from the building, having been warned off by the porter and the police, after several complaints.

The flat was actually in quite a good state and Jonathan had it back on the market after some initial refurbishment works. He needed the money and a quick profit would all help given his current lack of film work.

Some six months later Jonathan was at Christmas film party with Jack just off Soho, in Central London, when Jack pointed out a tall dark haired lady, dressed in black.

'That's her,' Jacks said pointing a finger across the room.

'Her who, Jack darling ?' asked Jonathan.

'The women with the flat in Belsize Park with the big metal door,' Jack replied.

'Gosh, the lead perhaps for our horror picture Jack. Perhaps a bit too close to home?' quipped Jonathan.

Suddenly, the tall dark haired woman dressed in black approaches Jack and Jonathan.

'Why hello Jack, how are you?' asked the woman

'Keres, this is Jonathan. He is a film director,' Jack kicked in.

'Keres, that's an interesting name, what does it mean?' asked Jonathan

'Oh, in Greek mythology, the name of the female 'death spirits'. But it is actually used quite a lot in modern Greece too,' replied Keres

'Interesting,' Jonathan said quietly.

Jack starts to move off to meet other people, leaving Jack in the lurch.

'And you are a film director. Goodness, I am merely a lowly actress, what are you working on at the moment?' Keres asked

'Actually a low budget horror film called 'Dracula's Daughter', we got green lighted last week. The first tranche of money came through yesterday. It is a low budget film which is the way things seem to be going these days. We go into pre-production next month,' Jonathan replied.

'What's the story line in this film?' asked Keres.

'Well it is a sort of re-make of a French film from the 1970's, an erotic horror film with a contemporary urban setting. A kind of new urban myth. The main location centres around a block of flats in North London. The main female lead gets re-possessed from her flat. Goes on the rampage, sells her soul to the devil, turns herself into a female vampire to seek revenge. A good old fashioned revenge and horror movie! These kind of movies always seem to make money. That's what people want.'

'Have you found your leading lady….Leading lady vampire yet?' asked Keres coyly.

'That's in Jack Fontaine's hands, whom I understand you know quite well and have worked with before,' Jonathan said starting to move off.

'Funny thing though Jonathan, I used to own a flat in Belsize Park. But I have moved on since then. Anyway, I would certainly be interested in your film, I will give Jack a call in the morning,' Keres said smiling in a sort of seductive way at him. Jonathan is beginning to think Keres looks like a vampire, with too much make-up on for any normal human being.

Jonathan makes as if to go, waves to Jack, and moves across the room.

'Holy shit, I think I am living my own horror film. Low budget crap...what a way to earn a living...' Jonathan mumbled to himself as he starts to leave the party.

Jonathan meets Jack on the way out

'So you met Keres then?' asked Jack

'Sure, pretty weird name Keres, means death spirits in Greek mythology,' Jonathan stated.

'Well, Keres knew all about you buying her flat,' Jack replied

'How the hell did she know, I did not tell her, given the circumstances,' Jonathan snapped back.

'Well, I sure as hell did not tell her,' Jack said.

'In any case I don't think she would be right for the part, if she calls you. See you,' Jonathan said waving goodbye to Jack, and hurrying off into the night and all that it beheld.

N.B. **Keres:**
Greek myth name of female 'death spirits', daughters of Nyx who is the source of evil. KER is the singular form and the name of a goddess of violent death.

LawnMower

At one time Michael had thought that a book of things would have been an interesting book to write or at least discover and read. In the 1970's & 1980's there had been fat tomes on the history of ideas & design books, but nothing very decisive about the history of things or everyday objects that can effect one's life. Or even certain things that have a bizarre or long history spanning many generations.

Michael had a special liking for old dining tables and fireplaces and the stories they could tell. He tried to surround himself with these sort of artifacts, giving himself a veneer of security from a harsh and tragic world out there. Sometimes he would pick up an object, like an old magnifying glass and think about its history, who had handled it, who made it, how many families had owned it and so on.

His father had been an antiques dealer, and as a small boy he had wandered around his father's antiques shop in the West End of London, cautiously treading the bare floorboards, studying fine porcelain and some fine art. Fine art it seemed to him, mostly had some pedigree, some history.

Michael tumbled down through the world and reached his fiftieth year, arriving in the suburbs of North London, namely West Hampstead living in a semi-detached house, built in the late nineteenth century, with his wife Catherine and their dog. Their two children, Mary and Alister were grown up and had just about left home.

Michael surrounded himself with his objects and ideas that he collected, from his things plus his hordes of books, quite a number of which he had only half read before moving on. In the knocked through sitting room he sat in an old chair that had been in his parents' attic room at home. It was important to him because, he had studied up in the attic when he was an older teenager, swotting over classic novels before moving onto existentialism and twentieth century novelists, like George Orwell, Virginia Woolf, EM Forster and Hemingway.

This is where he thought his intellect had been expanded if somewhat radicalized. This chair held meaning and life for Michael.

However, Catherine and Michael had started to think about moving out of London to the country. London seemed to be increasingly about impersonal shopping in supermarkets, car parking, and endless queues of traffic. The traffic seemed worst on Sundays now. When you wanted to go to an exhibition on a Sunday, you seemed to end up bumper to bumper down Marble Arch or up the Finchley Road. Not what Michael had in mind at all.

Also, the myth that something was happening all the time in London had sort of run out of steam. Catherine and Michael were not going to the theatre, cinema, restaurants or dinner parties all the time. Cable TV and Sky Sports featured fairly strongly on a daily basis. Michael said that London and its suburbs were like many villages all put together.

You could hang around in West Hampstead for weeks and not go anywhere particularly, except to the local shops, wine bar and possibly just out for a curry or pizza. Could be anywhere. Plus the Greek guy who ran the local grocery shop whilst wearing only a vest as a top, most of the time, was beginning to get on Michael's nerves. He was always asking Michael for advice, when all Michael wanted to do was buy some bananas, milk and bread.

On this basis, Michael concluded that provided he take his things and books with him, he could live anywhere, town or country. Well, certainly in the Home Counties anyway.

So Catherine and Michael started to look for a place out of town, but near enough to drive back or get the train back into London in under two hours. Everyone seemed to be on the move, they discovered once they stepped out of their door into the green North London leafy suburbs. They took special outings to view properties. They would gather up house brochures and details, make marmite sandwiches and a thermos of coffee, and sally forth with the dog in the back of the car for a day's adventure and snooping.

Their search was far and wide, including to the north and east,
Norfolk and Suffolk, to the South, Kent and Sussex, and to the West as
far Herefordshire.

They were hoping to buy a substantial property by selling up in London for a good price.

Often the owners of the properties showed Catherine and Michael round. Everyone seemed to be very pleasant and jolly, and very keen to be helpful.

Except for one rather strange couple who had a large Victorian vicarage on the outskirts of Ross on Wye in Herefordshire. The owner who said he was a film director but who seemed to be very busy renovating this property, ignoring the people who were working for him, was very pompous and sat himself in a regal chair whilst telling Michael that he could drive to London in under two hours, but suggested that Michael should not try this. The owner did not seem to care whether he sold the place or not, too busy with his film. Well that one went off the list of 'possibles'. Perhaps a little too far from London.

Their search continued for months, became a kind of frenzy or disease. Michael would phone up estate agents asking for their lists of properties, and then re-phone for selected brochures which would end up piled on the kitchen table. Once a week he and Catherine would go through the batch, editing and sorting. Then more phone calls and final arrangements for a visitation to a potential property.

After their Herefordshire experience, they decided to look nearer to London in Sussex. Sussex held fabulous memories for Michael, as he had played cricket there for some twenty five years, & still played an annual cricket match in a small village just outside Lewes town in East Sussex. On a late June evening, driving home back to London after winning a match, a few beers and a barbeque, on clear night with the South Downs reflected in the moonlight, it seemed like paradise to Michael.

So when a property brochure came in from a Lewes estate agent, indicating an old vicarage, near where Michael played cricket, Catherine and Michael were more than interested. It was not ideal, too expensive and needed an awful lot of fixing up. But Michael would have his things and books to cocoon himself during this transition.

Having viewed the property only once, Michael attempted to negotiate a deal on his mobile phone in the car park of a pub just near this old vicarage. Michael made the call, inspite of the fact that there was a bad mobile signal and the place smelt of chips and cooking fat, plus it had taken nearly three hours to get there.

When eventually Michael managed to speak to the estate agent, he was asked whether he could actually pay for the place, as there were other interested parties. This got up Michael's nose, and made him all the keener.

He indicated to the estate agent that he would have no problem raising the three quarters of a million pounds for the vicarage and its ten surrounding acres. His solicitor would be in contact in due course.

A second visit was arranged for a Saturday morning. It seemed that the property had been inherited and was owned by a sister, and brother who did not look too well. Everyone was very jolly, and Catherine & Michael were shown round what was a huge property on three floors, plus a fairytale garden that led to a small copse which one entered through a lovely old caste iron gate.

Michael noticed that the house needed a substantial amount of building work, but was not put off by this. After all it was a beautiful part of the country, Catherine and Michael would break out of London, have an adventure and possibly live happily ever after.

That was the beginning. The weeks dragged on whilst solicitors drew up contracts, checked out Land Registry details and mortgages were drawn up.

Catherine and Michael had found a buyer, a New Yorker who was working in the City, for their semi-detached house who was going to pay a good price, but even so this left a short fall of nearly a quarter of a million pounds which would have to secured by a mortgage. This had been arranged through a friendly mortgage broker who did not ask as many questions, as possibly other brokers might have done, especially seeing that neither Michael nor Catherine were in full time work anymore. So be it.

As the day of contracts exchange drew nearer, Catherine started to have fretful nights worrying about large mortgages and were they biting off more than they could chew. Michael told her not to worry, that they were buying a substantial property which could only go up in value over the years.

But secretly he did have his own anxieties too, maybe it was pride, down right stubbornness or the estate agent in Lewes who kept phoning him, that prevented Michael from reviewing the predicament that he was getting himself into. He thought things would pan out. At least there would be a lot more to do than in West Hampstead. A new vista, a new horizon beckoned.

After the contracts of sale were exchanged and the ten per cent deposit was paid over there was no turning back. The excitement started rising when the removal men arrived and started to pack their house up, the day before they were to move.

Michael had devised what he thought was a clever scheme for his things and books. He had organized a colour coded scheme, whereby a red label meant a box to their new bedroom, a yellow label meant a box to their new kitchen in their country house and so on.

They were just left with a bed and a couple of chairs only, for their last night in London. Michael felt strange without any familiar objects or things to look at, touch or books to read. Outside their small suburban garden which had had a large number of beautiful plants in various pots, looked denuded too. Too late now, onwards and upwards Michael told Catherine as they had their last meal in their local Indian restaurant.

Next morning started early with Michael fretting about where the removal lorry was, which was coming back again to load the last items aboard. As Michael came down the front steps of his house he noticed that somebody had been sick all over the bottom step, after a good night out. Typical he thought as he chucked a hot bowl of water over the smelly mess. Michael indicated to Catherine that they would not have to put up with this sort of thing anymore in their new place.

The removal truck arrived and the driver was given instructions on where to go and what time they should meet up outside their old vicarage in Sussex.

When Michael and Catherine got near to their destination, they felt hungry and stopped at a local garage on the road outside Lewes town. Michael made a phone call to their solicitor, only to find out that there was a slight delay in the completion of the sale. After a fretful sixty minute wait, and several frantic calls on the mobile they returned to Lewes to collect the keys to their new property.

As soon as Michael saw the first colour coded boxes being unloaded he started to relax. But not for long. Removal men although pleasant, cheery and hard-working have a way of abandoning you to your fate once they have finished their strenuous work. They wave goodbye and tend to leave you with a lot of boxes and your old furniture placed in new rooms. So the shock began for Michael. The house was so big that they seemed to be engulfed by it. There was only partial heating and it felt cold in the house. Also the last owner had died in it, Michael had heard.

Never mind, Catherine & Michael battled on and managed to get the bed made up and to cook a meal. Their bathroom was dilapidated and the bath was a ghastly green colour, but they were in beautiful surroundings and were not overlooked by any neighbours.

Michael began to feel slightly odd and hesitant. Everything seemed to be in confusion, stuff everywhere and he was going to attempt to renovate this house whilst living there.

On Sunday morning Michael told Catherine that he was going to take a cycle ride to get the Sunday papers. When he was out riding he passed one of the villages that was on the route to his annual cricket game. It did not quite seem the same now. It was late September, dark nights and winter days round the corner. As Michael cycled along to a garage near the main London to Bournemouth road to get the papers, he had a funny feeling that he had made a huge ghastly mistake. Everything about it started to feel awful and just not right. He thought that perhaps he needed to be more flexible and adapt, most things had an upside as well as a downside.

When Michael returned he parked his bike in the small stable block which was part of the property, and walked towards the house. He noticed all their beautiful potted urban plants had been lined up under a hedge all higgledy-piggledy, as if no one cared. It was so sad. Michael determined to make an effort in the garden, which could be nicely tidied up once he had got a proper lawnmower. The extent of the lawned garden suggested one of those sit on lawnmowers would do the trick.

So Catherine and Michael hunted through the local press ads and the yellow pages. They discovered that a brand new sit on lawn mower was more expensive than a good second hand car, some three to four thousand pounds at least. Wanting to work on a budget, they decided on a cheaper second hand one which seemed like a bargain at four hundred pounds. Only problem was that it was owned by someone who lived in Kent.

A white van was hired, together with two loading planks. Michael was given a demonstration of the machine in a small disused apple orchard in Kent by a pleasant old man who gave them some apples too. The lawn mower seemed to work just fine. The deal was done and the lawn mower was taken back to Sussex.

It had rained heavily on the way back from Kent. When they got back the cellar was completely under water. Michael panicked and rushed down there with a bucket and tried to bail it out. He noticed that the old central heating boiler was built up on a nine inch raised concrete plinth, suggesting that this flooding was a regular occurrence.

In his enthusiasm to buy the place Michael had persuaded Catherine that they did not need a full structural survey for this old crumbling run down property. They could see what needed doing. A valuation survey would be sufficient, and a lot cheaper.

Michael tried hard to remedy the situation albeit on a temporary basis. He cut all the ivy and brambles off the old caste iron gutters which ran near the cellar, hoping to clear things. He painted a couple of the smaller rooms, trying to get a modern trendy feel back in his life. He tried mowing the lawn, but it had suffered from rabbits digging it up in places. And just cutting some of the hedges seemed to take for ages, and all the potted plants seemed to lose their urban glory as autumn set in.

Unfortunately, everything that Michael put his hand to, did not seem to work down here. It was as if he was jinxed. In order to make the enormous drawing room feel warmer what better thing than a nice roaring log fire. Michael had found some old seasoned wood in one of the sheds. It was so hard that his flimsy chain saw broke down after a few attempts at chopping up logs. Sitting by a poorly lite fire is not really a good thing if you are trying to lift the spirits.

Also part of the property deal was that Catherine and Michael took on a mangy old Siamese cat, Saphira, that used to meow in a gruesome manner upsetting their old Spaniel dog Monty. Monty was loyal but this was not what he was hoping for, nor a cold room with a lousy fire.

There they sat the four of them, not much heating, a poor fire and winter coming on.

Michael had made up a one of the rooms into an office cum study with a telephone line and a computer. He was sitting there wondering what he should do next to better this situation, when he came across the brochure advertising the house, with the estate agents details.

Secretly he phoned the estate agent and gently enquired as to the state of the market. The estate agent was on to Michael immediately. He suggested that Michael might be missing London and his friends. Michael said that he might have to go to Australia for work, and therefore rather than attempting to let the house, they might want to sell it. Catherine and Michael had only been there for ten weeks.

Catherine was confused and shocked when he had told her what he was thinking of doing. To move back to London seemed like a crazy idea. But gradually the idea of having a front, with work in Australia that had suddenly come in, seemed like a plausible idea. Anything to stop Michael's current rantings. By now they were into October. Next the sale details were put up on the estate agents website. Unfortunately these things all take time.

Michael had started to feel that everything was falling apart. Many of his things and books were still in boxes in his make shift study. The house seemed more like a morgue to him than a fun place in the country. The local pub was used by coach parties for sing-alongs, and smelt of sweat, chips and grease.

The village shop appeared to be worse than the grocery shop he despised in West Hampstead. When Michael visited the pub on whose ground they played their annual cricket match, it appeared dark and cold with a few alcoholic locals just itching to sacrifice Michael for his folly.

Catherine suggested to Michael that maybe he should see a doctor, as he had not been sleeping well, & recently started blaming himself for everything. They visited a local doctor in Lewes, and after what Michael thought was an unsympathetic conversation was bundled out through the door with a subscription for Prozac anti-depressant pills, which made Michael feel giddy, sleepy and nauseous, certainly not better.

At the weekend Michael thought he would try to be positive and clear up the garden before the winter. He would have one final lawn mow, try to make the place nice to look out onto. Up and down he rode on the machine, bumping over rabbit holes, and anything else in his way.

Unfortunately the lawn mower which had started off alright when they had bought it, did not seem up to the amount of work Michael was putting it through. Maybe not man enough for the job thought Michael. It started coughing, back firing and going slower and slower. To Michael it was just another awful thing going wrong.

On his way back to the old garage where he stored it, the lawn mower gave up the ghost and stopped in its tracks, in the half light. Just as it was starting to get dark, Michael burst into tears, it was all too much. That night he could not sleep at all, he just keep going over one thing after another. It was all his fault, what did he think he was doing. He got up and went into one of the spare bedrooms which felt damp and cold. There did not seem to be any resolution to any of this.

The following day Michael thought he would go into Lewes and see the estate agent to find out if there was any interest in the house. When he got outside he found that his Volvo car had a flat tyre. Just another thing to deal with. Michael saw the estate agent with Catherine. There had been a couple of enquiries but no real interest.

More sleepless nights followed, and when Michael was not beating himself up mentally or blaming himself, he tried to read the Collected Letters of Evelyn Waugh. Fat lot of good that did him he thought.

Two days later the estate agent called Michael to say that a couple wanted to view the house. They arrived at late afternoon. Michael and Catherine had to do the selling, and telling the couple about Michael's new work in Australia. This couple looked vaguely familiar. Michael who was feeling all over the place, did not say a thing, on Catherine's suggestion. Catherine showed them round the garden. In his head Michael did not think this was a very good idea as the wife of the visiting couple had on very expensive looking half cut boots, the sort of thing one wore in Chelsea in London, not in the middle of nowhere as Michael was beginning to think of his new home.

The couple seemed interested but were non-committal. When they had left, Michael rushed up to Catherine and said he knew who they were. Catherine had no idea what he was talking about. Michael pointed out that they were the couple who had owned the vicarage in Ross–on–Wye, said he was in films or so he said, more like they must be professional vicarage restorers. Catherine thought maybe he was right and left it at that. Michael mumbled something about serial vicarage hunters.

Time ticked on with no interest in the property. It was mid-November. One morning Michael was doing a rough check list of what needed to be done to restore the house to its former glory.

He went outside and checked the roof tiles. He went back inside and went to one of the attic rooms for a closer inspection of the tiles, out of the attic window. To his horror it appeared that many of these old pantile roof tiles needed replacing. It seemed like another nail in this coffin, as Michael speculated wildly, as to how much all this would cost.

Michael appeared to be very depressed, as he and Catherine sat in their run down kitchen with an over hot Aga cooker, drinking tea and eating fruit cake, staring out the window looking down on the half mown lawn. Then the phone ran, the estate agent was sending over a couple to view the property. They had already sold their property in London and were cash buyers.

Michael appeared to be very defeatist and said they would never buy this wreck.

Catherine suggested that she handle things when they arrived. An hour later a Range Rover drove up the drive. Once they had arrived Catherine suggested tea and cake. Michael said he would make it. He was very nervous, and noticed that they were down to their last tea bags too. After tea and cake, Michael and Catherine explained that they would need to go to Australia for work and wanted to sell immediately as a result.

The couple said that they had just been 'gazumped' on the property they were going to buy down the road. They said they were desperate as they had three children in school. They did not know what to do. Suddenly, out of the blue, the women said that they loved Michael and Catherine's house, and wanted to buy it.

Michael who was feeling very negative about it all, said that there was a lot of work needed doing to the house. That was not a problem said the husband as his father was a builder and could solve most building problems. Plus he was not always working and would take it on as a project, whilst his wife continued running her post card business in London. He would look after the kids, once they had been placed in a local school.

Catherine had suggested to Michael to hold back on any negative comments about the house, before this couple arrived. So far Michael had been very quiet. However, when the conversation came round to surveys, he thought he was sunk. Not so. The couple asked Michael if he had had a structural survey. Michael said that he and Catherine knew the house needed a lot of work, and they had not bothered.

Michael said it was not falling down. The couple agreed and said they would not bother with a major structural survey either.

It seemed like salvation. But by the time another sale notice was arranged through the estate agent, Michael was in a bad way, thinking that this had all been his fault and was a complete waste of time and more importantly money.

Increasingly, he felt that he might need to see a psychiatrist, to see if there was any real cure for all his mental angst. His sleepless nights only seemed to make everything doubly worse. Catherine called their old doctor back in London, who suggested a specialist in a private clinic just off Marylebone Road.

Michael and Catherine went to see this psychiatrist who was quite old and very sympathetic. Michael thought that maybe he had been taught by Freud. It was suggested that Michael needed a good rest, and some psychiatric help to deal with all his problems. After a long and tortuous discussion with Catherine, Michael volunteered to spend some time in the clinic. If he wanted to leave he could at any time.

Michael was shown into a small bedroom with its own bathroom. Catherine sat on the bed, putting on a brave face. The psychiatrist came to visit and chatted with Michael for some time. Next a male nurse came in to offer Michael some calming drugs. Michael was very suspicious of drugs, and the Prozac experience in Sussex had not increased his belief in them. Eventually, after some time of playing cat and mouse with this male nurse, Michael swallowed his prescribed dosage. He started to feel enormously drowsy, and was soon asleep. He entered another world.

For the first week Michael caught up on his lost sleep. The drugs seemed to completely knock him out. The clinic was run more like a hotel, each patient coming out of their room and going down to the restaurant for meals three times a day, with quite good food.

Michael sat by himself in the restaurant but started to notice some of the other patients. Some appeared to be drug addicts, alcoholics, eccentrics, but quite a number appeared to be what Michael thought were fairly normal if there was such a term. Gradually Michael started chatting to some of them. A number of the patients seemed to go about the daily routine as if they were at school. However, Michael was wary of the lot of them. One woman Michael had lunch with raved on about medication throughout the lunch.

Michael had various friends visit him, and Catherine came every day, and their children. He made tea for them all, and chatted on about feeling better, and that it seemed rather like being in an ordinary hospital after an operation. Really just like recuperation.

Hiroko Minato, their Japanese next door neighbour from West Hampstead came to see Michael and gave him a Japanese style gown for relaxing in. Michael thought that although everyone was very worried about him, they were all putting on a brave face
.
Michael started to think again about why he was in here, and also more about some of the other people who had landed there temporarily.

The clinic organized various group therapy sessions, plus patients continued to meet up with their psychiatrist regularly. It was run rather like a college timetable. Everything regular and on time. There was a specialist Cognitive lecturer from London University who had published quite a number of books. In these Cognitive Behaviour Therapy sessions there were about twelve patients. CBT seemed to be all about being human, being able to make mistakes, but that it was not the end of the world if you made one.

Michael thought it sounded reasonable. It seemed like a mechanism to deal with the here and now, not some sort of Freudian or Jungian historical case study, into one's deepest childhood. He realized that he had just had made a huge mistake with his Sussex venture, and that was all. In these sessions Michael told the other patients about his folly and mistake. He felt better, relieved. But more to the point he discovered that he was not alone, by any means.

Michael discovered in his main Cognitive Behaviour Therapy session, there was an antiques dealer, a television presenter, a property developer, a lady who ran a veterinary practice, and a minor celebrity pop star who had been into everything apparently. From what he heard from them, Michael concluded that they had all over done it, by possibly attempting the impossible, certainly over doing it. Their mistakes were there for all to see. Michael thought this resulted in people blaming themselves, getting hugely depressed and not being able to work properly.

His conclusions were backed up by the talks, therapy meetings and by Michael's chats with his psychiatrist. The CBT seemed to give people mental and social tools to get control back into their lives.
Michael should not worry about all his things and books, it was his mind he had to clear of guilt and blame. To Michael this cognitive process seemed like a terribly effective therapy for an awful lot of mental stressed out conditions. The final comment Michael took from the therapist conducting the sessions was

'Don't awfulise things'

Michael did not know whether it was proper English, but it made sense. He had been doing that about everything recently. Nothing had seemed possible.

After a week of this Michael concluded that he needed to clear his head and to attempt to start again in the real world. The psychiatrist recommended another week, and Catherine thought he needed more time too. The problem for Michael was the strength of drugs he was being given which seemed to knock him sideways, and made him pretty drowsy, especially after breakfast in the morning.

There was a little gym downstairs which Michael went to when he started his second week in the clinic. Michael did various exercises, sweated profusely, and then went onto the running machine for five minutes which he found very difficult. But as he was leaving, Michael had a great feeling for a short time. His head felt clear. His mind seemed to be where it had been before all this house mistake had taken place. Then Michael felt drowsy again, and soon after dinner, the male nurse came round with another heavy dosage of drugs. A short while after Michael entered that other world again.

Michael chatted with Catherine about the changes that seemed to be happening to him. Catherine looked very tired, Michael knew she had been busy with the house sale in Sussex and finding somewhere to live back in London. Even so, Michael was fascinated by the fact that every time he went for a work-out in this little gym in the basement of the clinic, his head cleared and he felt renewed for a little while. He persisted for the whole week gradually feeling that he could leave the clinic soon and face the world again.

After fourteen days, the psychiatrist said that Michael was ready to leave. The senior male nurse provided Michael with a series of pills that he had to continue to take. Catherine had found a place to live in North West London again, not far from West Hampstead. The Sussex house sale was going through, and contracts had been exchanged.
Michael had already been out of the clinic once with his brother John and Catherine for a short period, for a Sunday lunch, and then returned to the clinic. But when he left the clinic for good, it was on a late November afternoon and it was already getting dark. The little house that Catherine had organized for them to stay in felt a little foreboding, it was new territory again.

Michael's dog Monty was waiting faithfully when they arrived at the little mews house with cars parked all around outside. The front door seemed to open straight onto the sitting room. It was tiny in comparison to the huge house in Sussex. Catherine helped Michael unpack and showed him where some of his things and books were. The rest had to go into storage. For once Michael did not seem to mind.

Over the coming weeks Michael and Catherine seemed to pick up the pieces and gradually settled back into London life, with Michael talking long walks with the dog on Primrose Hill or Hampstead Heath. He felt much better and had stopped taking the strong drugs prescribed by the clinic. They did not seem necessary any more.

Michael and Catherine started to see friends again and heard through the grapevine the odd comment about their rustic venture in Sussex. On comment seemed to be particularly telling. A friend of friend told them what their friend Peter had said. Peter who lived close to where they had owned the vicarage, was heard to say one night in the pub where they played cricket, commenting on Michael's and Catherine's arrival and subsequent rapid departure.

'Now's you see's them, now's you don't!'

Later Hiroko Minato their Japanese friend came to see them just before Christmas for a supper. Catherine had helped Hiroko with some legal problems, after her husband had died suddenly of cancer. They had always got on well together, there seemed to be some kind of unspoken bond between them. After a while during the supper Hiroko started to ask Michael about what had gone wrong in the country and why had they come back to London.

'What happened Michael really?' said Hiroko hesitantly.

'It's a long story actually,' said Michael quietly, whilst Catherine looked on sadly.

'Country no good then?' enquired Hiroko.

'Country no good Hiroko,' replied Michael.

'I see. Too much to do, too much lawn mowing then?' asked Hiroko.

'Especially if you buy cheap old lawn mowers,' Michael said smiling
and starting to laugh. Catherine nodded her head at Hiroko, looking somewhat sad and distant.

CHRIS SOMEBODY

Peter Rushton had worked for years in the film and television industry, mainly in London. According to his Cinema and TV Union ticket he was a Producer/Director.

After studying at a prestigious Film School, Peter had initially worked in the Middle East, setting up an Arab Television Station, and then in Nairobi, East Africa running a cinema commercials company which post-produced in London. On his return Peter settled back into London working mainly in Soho, in the centre of town, as a First Assistant director on film commercials and the odd feature film, plus the occasional free-lance contract in television arts programming. Peter had even got involved with a film and video distribution company to help pay the rent.

Then finally, he cut his teeth in a major post-production house, in central London where the very latest digital graphic design and editing computers were available. It was a steep learning curve. Instead of hanging around in a cutting room editing a commercial or a film, surrounded by bits of film and magnetic tape in bins, one now spent hours in an 'on-line cave', under the ground in front of lots of television monitors, paying heavily by the hour to hire these very expensive editing suite with a top flight computer editor, many of whom thought they were rock stars.

Suddenly everything went all electronic and computerized, and then digital. You just had to keep up with the technology or you were gone.

But behind all this struggle was always the ambition to direct features films. This was the highest accolade in the film business to be a feature film director. Peter was always coming up with good stories and ideas for feature films, hoping that he might be able to direct one of these stories. He pitched them to big production companies, even out to Hollywood producers and got precisely nowhere. But it felt good. However, down in central London in Soho, Peter was not alone. There were many other directors with similar tales of great scripts and then tales of woe, and getting nowhere fast.

In order to keep afloat and after a couple of lucky breaks, Peter become a television commercials director.

But he considered that he had sold his soul to the devil. Peter even asked one of his main TV commercials clients if he was Mephistopheles, to which he was told to 'fuck off' or they would get another director.

In Peter's mind, it was one stage behind being a feature film director, even if the films were only thirty or sixty seconds long, and normally pretty mindless, being based on selling products not on real art which was to be found in storytelling. He often shot on 35mm film and many of his crew members worked on feature films too. Out of all this mish-mash, getting so near and then so far from making a feature film, he was still driven to attempt to direct a feature film, and to raise money for a feature.

To this end, Peter and a casting director mate, Damian Clarke, were sitting in one of the more prestigious media clubs in Soho, the 601 Club, founded in the 1980's, with Peter going on about how difficult it was to raise money for an independent feature film, even if you had directors and producers with serious track records, a polished film script, good cast, crew and a reasonable budget.

'Bigger budget films over USD $10 million often lose money,' Damian suggested.

' Yes, but there are plenty of exceptions, where an independent film will make a fortune, especially for a distribution company if they get in early,' replied Peter.

'Point taken, but I know that you are more likely to get money for a low budget film, like a horror film or 'a gangster wrap' film where the million bucks or so for the budget, comes with less strings attached, i.e., the money is available, no pre-sales, domestic sales or completion bonds or guarantees from the Banks, and all that circus...'

'I guess. The Banks tend to think all films lose money which is just not right. The Banks don't mind acting as a facility once you have got the money, or making up the last piece of the financial jig-saw at vast expense and with heavy interest, knocking a big hole in the film budget rather than helping it. Or you sell out to the big studios in Hollywood.'

'Look here Peter, I could probably get you a film but it would have to be a low budget film, probably horror. And you write the script. Television takes them up, or to the DVD market, and downloading is starting to take over on distribution.'

'I see.'

'The last film I cast was horror, and was sold to television. Covered its budget comfortably. Why don't you view the horror TV Channels, and see what a ninety minute horror film is now made of?'

'Research up Satanism and make it commercial,' Peter says smiling to himself.

'Just do the research and we'll talk again when you have a decent film treatment to show the money guys,' Damian says firmly.

'OK.'

After Peter thought that he had researched and developed up a good enough film treatment of some twelve A4 pages worth of horror, he agreed to meet Damian again in the 601 Club to discuss the project.

They met just as it was starting to get dark. Damian had already received an email of the treatment. Peter was very keen to go through it with him and to talk up all the salient points. Damian starts to go through his copy of the treatment. Whilst Damian is reading through it, Peter is distracted by a lone older male, who enters the club in a grand theatrical manner. He is wearing a cloak and carries an ivory in-laid walking stick.

'All he is missing is the top hat,' Peter said quietly.

'Sorry...,' says Damian looking up from the film document.

'That's Chris, what's his other name....oh, Chris, Chris somebody ?' mumbled Peter.

Chris meantime has sat in a winged back armchair, sitting himself away from the club crowd. He just sits very upright and observes.

'He was quite a well-known director, in his time,' added Peter.

'I see, but shouldn't we be getting on,' asked Damian.

' Yes. Sorry. But actually….. unfortunately his wife died suddenly and he is not very well either. I think he used to work for a top American film company and was one of the hottest commercials director in London and New York, at one time.'

'Really, well he ain't doing it now,' snapped Damian.

'Amazing what happens to people!'

Peter takes the odd surreptitious look, staring into the corner, thinking that he recognized this Chris Somebody from perhaps some other place too. But to Peter, Chris looked a bit odd, as if the blood had gone from his body. Peter imagines that maybe he was the film industry's own Dracula, feeding off the fresh blood of the young aspiring directors at the 601 Club.

'Listen I think you need to polish this treatment, and make it more commercial, more ghoulish, less arty and then you will be ready to write the first draft script,' Damian said emphatically, trying to get Peter's attention.

'Sorry I was miles away, I beg your pardon. Once you start on this horror thing it gets you, you know.'

'Sure, let's meet up again when you are ready. Email me.'

'Will do and thanks for your help Damian. If this film makes money we could do a profit spilt on net points, once the backers and distribution company have been paid out.'

'That would be good, but I would not hold your breath on that one Peter.'

Over the coming autumn months Peter and Damian met up several more times at the 601 Club to discuss details regarding the final treatment and then the film script, plus talking over who might finance this film.

Whenever, they meet, Chris Somebody is always there, dressed in the same cloak, with his walking stick, observing or just staring. To Peter, Chris seems to be looking for something that has gone. This all begins to spook Peter Rushton, who starts to have weird dreams about Chris and his horror film treatment.

Another month goes by, with lots of emails and potential for getting the film financed by two high net worth individuals, who are looking for some sort of tax deal or break. Peter and Damian hold a meeting with the two wealthy investors, to discuss their interest in the film, and potential film deal. During the discussion, Peter looks up and across the 601 Club.

Chris Somebody is seated quietly on the other side of the club, away from the crowd. He just looks on observing. After an hour or so Chris gets up to leave. Somewhat exasperated Peter gets up too, making out to Damian that he wants a pee. Chris brushes past Peter who nods at Chris. Chris just stares at him coldly. Peter notices that Chris has tears in the corner of his eyes.

'God, Christopher Lee, Peter Cushing and Gloria Holden all rolled into one,' mumbled Peter to himself.

Other guests in the 601 Club stare at Peter as he begins to move off towards the door.

'What's that you're saying ?' says one of the film investors.

'Oh, just thinking aloud about old film directors....,' replied Peter.

'Really...'

Peter also harbours dark thoughts about film directors. He sometimes thinks they are like rats in a sewer, all attempting to climb up the media drain pipe, all thinking they are special, as in the film *'Ratatouille'*, rats everywhere but only one special rat in the end.

A week later, Damian and Peter hold another meeting with the two investors. Things are beginning to look good, but no contracts have been drawn up or heads of agreement been signed yet. But at least it appears that the investors like Peter's script.

However, on entering the 601 Club, Peter's first thoughts are about whether Chris will be there or not. Chris's usual winged arm chair in the far corner is empty. A little later on, an overweight producer with an American accent takes the seat, and starts talking loudly.

Ten days later Peter and Damian meet to talk about what sort of deal they can expect if these rich investors fund their horror film. Final details before the deal is struck.

Peter looks around the club. No Chris. Peter cannot stand it. He goes straight out to the reception area of the 601 Club, and asks about Chris.

'When was Chris the director last in the club ?'

'Chris who?' asked Nancy, the nearest receptionist on the desk.

'Chris…er, Chris Somebody, what's his name, you know the director?'

'Yes..?'

'Chris... he wore a cloak, carried an inlaid walking stick, looked a bit anaemic, bit like Dracula on a good day.'

'Oh, I am thinking you might be talking about Chris Lane, the director,' Nancy suggested.

'Yes him,' Peter whispered to himself.

'Chris Lane has been dead for at least two years now. First his wife and then Chris. Very sad really,' Nancy stated sadly.

'What?' Peter shouted out.

'He was a great director in his time, so I have heard, in commercials and made some feature films too,' Nancy continued on.

'Thanks, I have got to go....,' Peter declared and rushes outside into the night for some fresh air.

On the opposite street corner, some tramps and hobos sit or lie, next to a pile of plastic rubbish bags. Peter remembers that when he was younger, the standing joke with his film buddies, was that this street corner was where old film directors ended up, in amongst the rubbish.

'Maybe Chris is with those guys now,' Peter thought to himself.

'Could be joining that lot soon myself, if this bloody horror film does not happen.'

Somebody rushes past Peter, bumping into him and nearly knocking him over.

'You alright mate? Want to watch where you are going,' the stranger said.

'Sure...sorry. Just thought I saw a ghost.'

'What in Soho? You must be kidding, full of hookers, drunks and clapped out film directors!' The stranger said quickly disappearing into the city night.

N.B. Ghost:
1 n. apparition of dead person or animal, disembodied spirit; emaciated or pale person; shadow or semblance (*not the ghost of a chance*) ; secondary or duplicated image in defective telescope or television-picture. **2.** v. act as ghost writer (of, for). The Pocket Oxford Dictionary Seventh Edition 1984.

Foreign Places

(Below are extracts taken from an old 1980's diary found in a North London suburb, when a house was emptied before being refurbished):

'It was very underplayed everywhere. My father was originally from Sudetenland, Czechoslovakia, having left in 1919 after the First World War ended. He had starved in the First World War He came to Richmond in London and could not speak a word of English.

He had left all his family behind. Made his way from there. He was just eighteen. What a guy!

After the end of the Second World War all his family who had remained there in Sudetenland, being German speakers, were all kicked out or escaped, and fled to Bavaria in Southern Germany. From my earliest memories as a child, the idea was that we would visit our relatives near Ulm in Southern Germany. The first trip we took was in 1948.

On these annual trips there were my three older brothers and my father. My mother never came on these trips. Taking a Cross Channel ship was like something out of an old Navy War film. Believe it or not, they even had trains on the lower deck which were all chained down. This was fascinating for a four year old boy, well into his steam engines, and the beginnings of a Hornby Double 'O O' train set love affair.

'The Old Man' or Tom as we called our father, cooked up lots of boiled eggs and made various sandwiches, before we left. Feeding us lot was an expensive exercise.

Having arrived in northern France at Dunkerque port, on the early morning Channel crossing at about 4 am, still in darkness, my father would attempt to drive the whole way to Bavaria without staying in a hotel. This meant crossing into Belgium, up the dual carriageway to Brussels onto Aix La Chappelle or Aachen, then hitting the Autobahns to Frankfurt,

Stuggart and then South East Germany on the Munich road.

No English seaside holidays for us lot, just bombed out Germany by the sea first and then inland where the whole country seemed have been bombed flat.

Inspite of enormous war damage, with towns still piled up with rubble, bullet and mortar shell holes everywhere, nobody had seemed to have blown the autobahns up much or they had been re-built very quickly after the War. Also, the Autobahns were amazing pieces of road engineering or so it seemed to us boys from war damaged England.

Everything else seemed to have been bombed. In the distance you would see blown up bridges, shattered buildings, many covered all over with bullet holes. There were poor people everywhere, and not much of a smile amongst them.

Germany had a re-building tax added on to all goods and services. But people seemed friendly enough. I suppose they were not the Nazis, who had all run away or were in hiding, or saying that they were not responsible for what happened. Some of the Nazi leaders had been tried and hanged. But not all of the SS commanders and soldiers, by any means.

But for us kids it was a bit of a game, it was always Brits versus the Germans. We played all these war games at our boarding school. Pretending you were a Spitfire fighter plane was a good one, rushing around the play-ground with your arms out stretched like plane wings, making machine gun noises as you ran past each other. But in Germany we were seeing it for real.

Thus the Autobahns became a serious part of our holiday life, as we seemed to spend interminable hours on them, checking signs and distances for my father who was often just trying to keep awake. They also seemed to be much more modern than anything we had in England. Amazing what forced labour can do.

I not sure whether after the Bretton Woods Allies Meeting in 1944, it was decided to pump huge amounts of reconstruction money into Germany including repair of the Autobahns, but they all seemed to work. There were decent laybys, no speed limits and good garages with cafes. There were also huge double length trucks wheezing along. I used to try to count the number of wheels on these rigs. At that time amongst other things I wanted very badly to become a truck driver.

It was difficult for four boys, or sometimes three of us, if Tony my eldest brother did not come along, to keep still, on such long journeys.
There were always minor fights, Dad telling us to quieten down, and endless questions to my father about when we going to stop for a drink and a pee. Dad was on a mission, so all that had to wait.

This was post war continental driving. You had to have your GB plates on the car. You might see a very occasional other British car whom everybody waved to. However, any vehicles that vaguely looked like German army vehicles we furtively gave the V-sign to, from the back window of our car. During this time American troops and transport trucks were everywhere in Germany. Again more fascination for us, American trucks and Americans were not like anything else we had seen before.

My father could speak fluent German, French and English, so being in Germany was not a problem for him. For us kids it was, though we were taught French at school, German was not on the syllabus. So there was that stumbling block when we wanted to say something or even attempt to buy anything. We had to ask my father to translate, which seemed to give him a lordly position on any linguistic proceedings.

One year we took my mother's father, Papa who was from Buhl near Baden Baden in Strasbourg. He was a tall elegant nineteenth century looking man with a goatee beard who had left Buhl before the First World War, now lived in North London round the corner from us in West Hampstead, and worked in Baker Street as a trichologist whom we thought was something do with the circus till we were older. Anyway Papa convinced my father that there was a short cut to Baden Baden, via a bridge over the Rhine.

After what seemed like an interminable time going across country, stopping, asking the way in German, we spotted this bridge as the sun was going down and we were all starving. It turned out that the bridge had been blown up, so we had another detour. We thought it had been blown up in the Second World War. In fact we found out later that it had been during the First World War!

That night we stayed in the main Hotel in Buhl before the town had been by-passed, with great double length trucks roaring past outside the window. We were happy to be there, and there was a wedding festival on, plus some sort of fair. One of my eldest brothers Chris or Tony managed to shoot a fair organizer in the bottom with an air rifle used for shooting ducks off a row. Much German consternation.

Buhl was a lovely old Alasce town with a church in the middle, with a stork nesting on top of the church tower, the like of which we had never seen before. They had traditional plum pudding and there seemed to be much discussion about the Black Forest. My grandfather seemed to remember some of his old mockers from before the 1914, and got himself and my father invited to this wedding. We went to bed in disgust, spitting out of the Hotel window on to passers-by.

Next morning, my father was very quiet, it had been a good wedding reception. My father took us to Baden Baden swimming pool which was superb with a really high diving board. Certainly, my father did not seem himself, and wanted to rest and keep quiet for most of the day. The old driving force to get to Bavaria and his sisters and brothers in law, seemed to have gone for the day. My father was not a big drinker, and I realized that he must have had a hangover. He was not himself. Quite a shock, my father liked his wine but was not a big drinker by any means. He left that sort of thing to some of my uncles.

Next day we were back on the Autobahn, hammering along after a lengthy packing of the car which always seemed to take forever. Getting to Bavaria was always exciting, as my aunts lived next to Alps which you could see quite clearly in the distance through the lovely green lush fields with docile cows with bells round their necks, clanking away. My auntie Mary lived at first in temporary accommodation, it must have been a refuge complex, even had 'dunnies,' a nice wooden seat and a hole in the ground. People used old newspapers. This was at a small town called Marktoberdorf, not far from Kaufbeuren and Fussen, and the city of Ulm on the River Danube, and the Munich Autobahn.

My auntie had fled from Russian Communist occupied Sudetenland, with my cousin Susie who was same age as me. They had come through some sort of American protected corridor which was an escape route, all done running through the night with the occasional live round being fired at them. So we heard. All sounded pretty dramatic to us boys from

North London suburbs. These trips often lead to other trips too.

On one of these other trips, my father had driven to Vienna with us boys and my cousin Susie, who looked like Rachel Welch, the film star, and whom I had a secret crush on. Vienna looked like something out of a black and white movie with the Harry Lime theme playing, and spies everywhere you looked. The city was controlled by the Russians, the Amercians and the Brits. It was dark and sombre when we arrived at night. Not much joy around, just lots of sinister shadows.
Intimidating, until we saw a restaurant with the same name as our surname. It looked expensive. It was expensive, the waiters were all still going around with long tail dining suits and the restaurant was grandly lite by many chandeliers. Vienna old style. The diners were equally elegant. We boys were in our khaki shorts from boarding school! My father was persuaded to let us go in. The restaurant had the same name for goodness sake!

We caused quite a stir among these bourgeoisie Viennese who seemed to have got off lightly, after all their fascism and war-monging they had been involved in. But we all had a great meal and it was a most memorable moment for me. It was 1948.

Anyway, seeing my aunt and cousin meant the end of a long psychological journey, as one of my earlier memories was to drip sealing wax onto food parcels which were sent to my Czech relatives. I must have been small, as I can remember standing on the kitchen table carefully dropping the wax on to the string knots with my mother co-ordinating the operation. So here in Bavaria, was where all the parcels went.

It was a very jolly affair, with my auntie Mary and her sister Heidi and her husband Rudi, my cousin Susie who looked like Rachel Welch, and a big playful Alastian dog called Rex. Mary's husband had been killed in a car crash after the war. We found out that his surname had been Rummel, as in the German General who had made life very difficult for the British troops in North Africa in the War. It was another thing that seemed a bit odd, to have a relative with a German General's surname.

But it all seemed par to the course, as my father's original Christian name had been Adolfus, which he had changed to Anthony when he came to England. We boys had found this out one day when we were climbing around in the old spare bedroom which was full of junk.

We found my father's old violin and its case with his full name written onto the inside cover. My father had lived for a while in Paris, then after for a short period in London, and then New York. I think it was his attempt at being musical at the time. Get the fiddle out. I can see why he changed his name to Anthony. All a bit confusing for a youngster holidaying in Bavaria!

So out of the car we get after a very long journey, welcomed with many kisses and hugs and a totally incomprehensible language.
Inevitably, we started to pick up some German, but it was not easy. These visitations were all about food and socializing over a week or ten days.

As relatively conservative youngsters we noticed the different food that people ate. For breakfast in London we had Cornflakes and boiled eggs. In Bavaria, my auntie gave us cold grilled breaded veal, 'weinersnitchel', and a type of sponge cake with a hole in the middle. What do you do, you do not want to say no, but the food is treated suspiciously as if your relatives are trying to poison you. It all turned out alright and I still have a secret longing for cold 'weinersnitchel' in the morning.

The other odd thing was my aunt used to keep this cold cooked veal in a chest of drawers which must have acted as a temporary cool storage cupboard. Put all the elements together, and it is a little surprising for a young London kid used to his cornflakes.

We had no real fixed idea about it, but I think they were all glad to be alive. That was the main thing, before the pressures of a renewed bourgeois existence took over again, this funny world in Bavaria that we travelled to, seemed to hold a kind of romance for us together with the snowy Alps clearly visible in the background. Not like bombed out London at all.

Also my mother and father seemed to nearly re-enact the Second World War at our home in London, huge rows and much door slamming, with two very strong personalities trying to work out their destinies in post war middle class Britain, especially with rationing books and everything else.

My mother tended to stay at home when we went on these trips to war torn Europe to visit our newly discovered distant relatives.

So for us boys there were no huge rows to steer round in Bavaria, with its different but broader horizons. It did not seem to matter, even though we could not speak the language......!'

La Dona Suena

Spanish Meaning for:
La Dona:*Used as a courtesy title before the name of a woman in a Spanish-speaking area. Placed before a name to indicate respect.*
Suena:*from the Spanish verb* ***Sonar to dream*** *present tense: 'she dreams'=* ***Suena*** *.*
Free On-Line Dictionary

Terry Martin was what you would call all over the place and not in the first flush of youth. In fact he was well past it. It made no difference though. After a declining career in film and television production, joining what Terry thought was the rest of them, he had headed for some property development in North West London which was his manor.

Then Terry had another brainstorm, why not get a place in the country too, so that any property renovation or maintenance in London would take twice as long and be twice as expensive with all the traveling in and out of London! Terry had once done up a small mews property off the Goldhawk Road in West London, and whilst waiting for the rush hour traffic to die down before returning to East Anglia, had sleep amongst the rubble bags and on some left over insulation on the floor. Felt quite comfortable too. So at that time all seemed possible one way or another.

Currently, Terry had two flats in a block of flats in Belsize Park which were extremely good to rent out, location, location and all that. Even so Terry thought it was a bit like some American clapped out 1930's block or the Hotel Californian in the 1940's with Raymond Chandler types hanging around every corner or by the 1950's antiquated lifts.

He had had a one bedroom flat at the back of the block overlooking the communal gardens, for ten years now. He had decided years ago outside a pub in

Southwold on the Suffolk coast, when he had a hot sale offer on this flat, that he would keep it instead, treat it as an economic exercise, and see what he could make of it. It had worked, he had borrowed against it to pay off some nasty lawyers bills, to fund his life style, i.e., to just keep going, and to carry out some home improvements. And it always rented well. There were very few vacant or 'void periods' as it was called in the rental business.

So when the chance of a small studio flat in the same block, came up for sale at a knock down price, he thought it was too good to refuse, especially as he had some money left over from his original sale of his home in London and the move to East Anglia. Although being over sixty five years old, Terry was in there with his paint brushes one cold January weekend, and got the flat painted up to a good standard. It rented out immediately to a Spanish au pair who was looking after a family in a big house in Hampstead, or loads of money....

Jolly good thought Terry, but he had always been slightly intrigued about who his tenants were, what they looked like, what were their ambitions and careers. That was, as long as they paid the rent, and did not wreck the place.

In fact the first tenant whom Terry had rented his first flat to, had done exactly that, after a while no rent and he semi-wrecked the place.

Terry was still living in London, just round the corner then. The tenant had had an impeccable reference from a judge, produced a bank statement that showed he had over £77,000 in his current account, and had been working in IT for a supermarket chain. Just the sort of tenant Terry thought he wanted as the flat had been newly refurbished with wooden floors throughout and beautifully decorated.

My, how things can change. The tenant turned out to be a bit of a coke head, was fired from his job, and started 'action painting' in the flat. And that was just the beginning, he started not to pay the rent on time, insisted on bringing it round by hand to where Terry was living, always late. Occasionally, he gave off a whiff of potential physical intimidation towards Terry.

Then there followed a formal complaint from the management company of the flats, stating that a woman had been seen late at night in the garden, outside his flat, screeching and yelling, and breaking windows. Apparently it was this guy's ex-wife or girlfriend.

Next the rent stopped being paid. The whole thing was taken over by the local council of Camden who were going to pay the rent instead, whilst they were preparing to re-house this guy who had a baby girl and was therefore eligible for council housing. Seemed like a bit of a scam to Terry, especially when the council said they would pay the rent whilst his dodgy tenant was re-housed.

Shortly afterwards the tenant called Terry up, asking him round. Nothing ventured nothing gained thought Terry. When the tenant opened the door, the flat was hardly recognizable, rubbish everywhere ,
a couple of broken chairs and ruined decoration.

Terry thought I would love to kill this bastard tenant, but realized that the only way that this mess could be sorted out, was for the tenant to leave. A few friends of Terry had suggested going round there, and physically throwing him out. Terry kind of agreed, but thought this was possibly silly macho stuff, definitely not the way forward what with all the health and safety regulations and the local council's involvement now, and looming court proceedings.

What the tenant had asked Terry round for, was to see if he could sell him some of his crazy paintings, thinking that he was a rich landlord type. The tenant did not seem worried about back rent, legal proceedings against him or the ruined state of the flat.

'What do think of this painting?' Was his first question to Terry, no mention of unpaid rent or an apology.

'Not my style,' Terry replied, quietly observing the tenant, whom he decided was completely deranged or had turned to Satan or was just on drugs as usual.

'OK sorry to bother you! I thought you might be interested.'

'Sorry. See you then.'

Terry decided it was time to go, before he was further compromised or he lost his rag.

All Terry had to do was get the conniving git out of his flat. Easier said than done. He would have to get a court order from a judge first. Time and money. In the meantime Terry would sometimes see this tenant in the local pub, usually stoned out of his brain.

One day in September, after a short holiday in the Mediterranean, Terry was walking down the street when he walked past the tenant in the street.

Thinking it better not to aggravate him, whilst the court proceedings were being processed, Terry just nodded to the tenant as he passed him outside the block of flats where Terry rented out the flat.

'Nice sun tan…,' the tenant said rather sarcastically.

Terry thought he was being accused of having a lovely life, and going on foreign holidays was all part of that. He started to feel guilty. Talk about changing the goal posts. The tenant seemed not to feel guilty at all. Terry reflected on one of his school boy economics aphorisms that 'all property is theft.'

The court order came through, that was sent to the council, they paid the back rent owing, the tenant was re-housed and the flat was empty again. Great.

Over the next few years, a series of tenants passed through, all different but none like the first. Occasionally, Terry would have to visit the flat during a tenancy to check out a problem, usually plumbing, including a big flood from upstairs. One eastern European tenant who had paid cash for six months in advance, had had alcohol optics installed onto the 1930's shelving. Another belonged to the Poetry Society with many high-brow, and possibly pretentious tomes strewn around the flat, but wanted to pay a low rent.

And then there was the daughter of a Swedish journalist, who seemed to be a photographer with a German boyfriend studying for a business degree in London.

This lady sounded very sympathetic on the mobile phone, when she asked for a number of boxes to be collected plus a few pieces of furniture that they did not need. They had already asked for the bed to be moved out before they moved in. Terry met her, a large somewhat over weight young lady dressed in black wearing a small fascinator hat, with a few tattoos on her arms. Terry thought she must be what they call a Goth. Her German boyfriend had a ring in his lip. They talked about photography for a little while. Then Terry collected the boxes and left.

What he had noticed was that the flat was full of new gothic type furniture, mostly black, posters on the walls, and generally pretty cluttered.

After nearly two years' tenancy, the Goths were going to return home. Terry's immediate thought was what about all that furniture. But the tenants asked if they could leave the new bed, television and other furniture. As Terry was pretty reasonable, and they had been good tenants, he agreed to this.

When Terry arrived with his wife Mary to check out the now empty flat, and carry out any required decoration, they found that they could not move for heavy black bookcases, cabinets, shelving, a second hand chest of drawers, a wonderful new big bed, plus a monster Sony television.

'What the hell are we going to do with all this stuff, a tenant won't be able to move in here?' yelled Terry.

'Calm down,' Mary quipped.

'Well I am going to start taking this stuff out of the flat, leave it outside, and go from there. At least we will be able to move about in here to do the decorating.'

'I have got an idea, why not take the furniture down to the front hall, put a sign up which says 'Free, help yourself' and see what happens,' Mary suggested.

'Brilliant Mary, just brilliant as usual,' said Terry smiling and heading for the main hall foyer with the first piece of furniture.

After about two hours Mary went down to check out what was happening. Most of the furniture was gone, including some heavy IKEA bookcases. However, a young lady was standing next to one of the last pieces, the chest of drawers. She told Mary that she was in a studio flat upstairs, that she had recently split up with her boyfriend, and that this chest of drawers would make such a lovely piece for her new flat. Mary waited for her and made sure she got the chest of drawers up to her flat, before anybody else had it.

Terry thought it had all worked out OK in the end, feeling good that he had not tried to sell the extra furniture or had it removed. He felt a vague sense of giving and generosity.

So when Terry was about to buy a second flat in this block he had thought about some of these previous tenants, weighing up whether it was worth all the hassle to buy another flat to rent.
With the current economic depression and very low rates of interest, a collapsing Eurozone, and a volatile stock market, Terry decided that investing further, in a little studio flat in this block, was a good investment or what landlords called 'producing a good return' with not so much risk. Just what he needed.

It so happened that Terry was the block of flats, very early one Sunday morning, having started out from

East Anglia, in the third week of September. It was still very hot with an extended Indian summer in most of England. Terry had come in, to quickly paint a bathroom ceiling in the first flat that he owned, at the back of the block, before new tenants moved in.

As he carried decorating stuff through the foyer hall, he could see the door of his new studio apartment, that he had recently acquired, which was now let to the Spanish au pair. Should he introduce himself, Terry thought to himself.

'Better not, against the rules really. Can't just turn up on her doorstep,' was what he concluded.

He was still intrigued though. He noticed an Amazon book delivery outside the studio front door. She probably was not in anyway, out working up in Hampstead.

The day progressed and got very hot indeed for London, up in the nineties. Terry ended up decorating without his T-shirt on, and got covered in paint drops. He cleaned up and then had to go 'buying' up at the Homebase Centre in Swiss Cottage. The usuals: shower curtain, some tile grout and silicon for sealing the shower edges, and a couple of light bulbs and a battery for the smoke alarm.

When he got back, Terry got a cold drink and a sandwich round the corner, had a good look round and thought this is what urban life is all about, all the young people hanging out in the cafes and bars, and all the old people struggling up the hill with plastic bags to get home or standing around chatting about nothing in particular.

Thinking it was time to get back to work, Terry made his way to the entrance of the block of flats somewhat reluctantly in all the heat. It was that time in the afternoon when it was hottest and without a breath of air.

It reminded Terry of being in Madrid in the summer when he was
a student years ago, on a very hot day at the famous Prado Fine Art Museum. He had seen a crowd of English female tourists who instead of being overwhelmed by the Goyas, Reubens and El Grecos on display, were simply overcome by the heat, and kept fanning themselves with their Prado Museum brochures.

As Terry approached the double entrance to the foyer of the flats, he let a Spanish looking woman go in before him. She was gently fanning herself.

'It is so hot today,' she said in a Spanish accent.

'Very hot,' Terry said.

Terry slowly entered the building and noticed that this elegant tall lady headed towards his newly acquired studio flat.

All sorts of thoughts started to go through Terry's mind. She looked a little too old to be an au pair, more like thirty five plus, and to be living in this studio flat. She looked distinguished and elegant, possibly even aristocratic.

Terry's imagination started to get carried away. She must be from Castile, possibly Madrid too, a maiden thwarted in love. Or even a young women looking out of for a possible suitor, but trapped behind 'la reja' or the iron grilles placed over the lower windows of houses, as in the days past in olden Catholic Spain, with Don Quixote riding along on the horizon, as the windmills quietly turned.

Images from older Spanish writers whom Terry had studied as a student, such as Garcia Lorca, Camilio Jose Cela, Pio Baroja and Cervantes flashed before his eyes. Definitely Don Quixote country!

Terry came to his senses when the tall elegant lady went to open the door to her studio flat off the main foyer. His studio flat. Instead of rushing over and introducing himself as he would have done twenty years earlier, he just bowed slightly towards her and continued down the corridor to his other flat and work in progress.

'La Dona whatever...,' Terry whispered to himself thinking he was dreaming a little.

'La Dona suena, that's it,' he said aloud.

'As in a dream...'

Terry got back to work and sweated away adding all the finishing touches so that he could get this rental flat completely ready for the new tenants.
He finished early and thought that he would get back to the country sooner rather than later as it was so hot. London could be murder in the heat. So he then had to clear all the paint, dust sheets and step ladder out of the flat again. It all had to be taken back through the hall again and loaded into his car outside.

As Terry was doing this, while thinking that the worst part of decorating was carrying all the gear in and out, he passed an Asian mother with a large modern pram, and a couple of suitcases, starting to load them into the lift in the front foyer of the block. Then he saw a little baby girl sitting on the floor, next to the pram. Next, he saw the father come out of the lift and head towards the foyer door presumably to get more stuff in, they were probably back from holiday.

When Terry came back into the foyer with the remainder of his gear he saw that the baby was on its own still sitting by the lift. Terry thought that was how babies went missing, but assumed that the mother or father was coming back from their car parked just outside.

Terry left, jumped into his car and drove off through the suburbs of North London, pleased that he had managed to do the decorating work, even though he was well past it age wise. But he found he still was thinking about the Spanish lady, the au pair of thirty five years plus, his new tenant.

'La Dona suena, La Dona suena,' Terry said aloud.

'What is she dreaming about, a man, a husband? No?'

'A baby. She was a spinster, cheated in love. She wanted a child more than anything in the world....yeah, yeah a real Spanish tragedy,' declared Terry to himself.

When he got home it was still very hot. Mary asked how it had gone, Terry said well, and he also told her about 'La Dona suena,' and his ideas of a Spanish tragedy.

'She's just an au pair for God's sake, and what on earth does 'La Dona suena' mean in any case?' Mary said firmly.

'Sort of aristocratic lady. 'Suena' means as in a dream. Found in classical Spanish tragedy, more recently in Garcia Lorca's plays, and all that.'

'I see'

'OK. I'll think I have a drink, do you want one?' Terry said shuffling off towards the fridge.

Terry thought no more about it. His other flat was duly rented out the next week, with the new tenants moving in on the Wednesday.

In order to keep up with the local news in North West London, and more particularly in Belsize Park where he had his flats, Terry had the local newspaper sent to him each week, as well as looking at it on-line. It had all the local news, reviews, latest restaurants and a section on property prices and flat rentals.

Sometimes, whilst Terry flipped through this paper he felt he had never really left North London. Maybe that's what he wanted or dreamed of. All he had to do was to reinvent himself and become young again.

As Terry went through the local news section, he noticed an article with a bold headline:

Baby girl goes missing in block of flats in Belsize Park.

Terry scanned down the article and noticed it was in his block, on the same day as he had been there.

'Oh my God, it's her,' Terry shouted out loud.

'What are you talking about Terry. Who's her?' asked Mary.

'La Dona suena, that's who.'

'Not that Spanish tragedy stuff again,' quipped Mary.

'Never mind Mary, this is serious.'

Terry read the rest of the article. It said that various tenants in the block had been interviewed. The police said that they had been especially interested in the ones who lived nearby the lift in the foyer of the block of flats.

Apparently, a Spanish au pair had been a possible suspect, as she had told some of her neighbours, that she had been married but could not have children and that her husband had run off with another woman who could. After questioning her and searching her flat she was released and cleared of any suspicion.

The article said that the mother and father were questioned too. Apparently, it was an arranged Asian marriage.

It appeared that the baby girl had been snatched from the block of flats by a relative and taken back to the grandparents' home in West London, as there had been a big family row on their recent holiday. The police were continuing their enquiries.

'La Dona suena, wherever happened to you?' sighed Terry, putting the paper down, and looking out of the window into the far distance.

'In Segundis'

nulli secundus
Second to none.
second
secondarily
secondary
1. Belonging to the second class in respect of dignity or importance; entitled to consideration only in the second place. Also, and usually, in less precise sense: Not in the first class; not chief or principal; of minor importance, subordinate.
2. Subsidiary, auxiliary; that which is used only in the

second resort, or that serves to assist something else.
3. Belonging to the second order in a series related by successive derivation, causation, or dependence; derived from, based on, or dependent on something else which is primary; not original, derivative.
4. Belonging to the second stage in a process of compounding or combination; consisting of two primary elements.
5. Short for secondary school or secondary modern school.

secondigravida

A woman who is pregnant for the second time.

Secondly

The above is part of what I ended up with after I went on the internet to find out what 'in secundis' actually meant.

The reason I was looking into this was because of something that had occurred when a friend came to visit for the weekend.

The weekend had started off well with a dinner party on the Friday with various people arriving from London and locally to my house in Suffolk. Saturday morning was quiet, but my friend Jonathan from London, had a problem, something to do with the exhaust on his small Korean car.

'Sounds like a mixture between a racing car and a tank,' Jonathan announced over breakfast.

'Well let's take it into Paul's garage down the road, you know Paul, we have just done a famous deal on a VW Golf with him and his brother Stephen. Good couple of blokes, great mechanics,' I suggested.

'OK, but I don't trust most garages,' said Jonathan.

'Oh come on for Pete's sake Jonathan, they're not even bothered about that pile of Korean crap anyway,' I snapped back.

'Speak for yourself. Right, bacon and eggs all round. Diana and you
Chris?'

'Good for me'

'Diana?'

'No thanks, just toast and coffee'

Later Jonathan phones the garage and Paul and Stephen agree to see Jonathan at 1.30 pm when they are not so busy. I walked the dogs, and Jonathan went for a separate longer walk, agreeing to meet up back at the house at around 1.15 pm.

Jonathan gets in the car, starts revving it. I get all excited at the throaty noise, hold my handkerchief up like the chequered flag at a race car meeting, open the gate for Jonathan who roars off down the road. I follow in hot pursuit.

When I get to the garage which is open with lots of cars in the service area, plus the office is open too, there is no one around. I walk up to Jonathan

'Looks like the bloody Marie Celeste, Chris old chap.'

'Maybe they are hiding from you and your car Jonathan.'

'Bollox….they're around somewhere.'

Jonathan and I go into the office. Nobody. I begin to think that maybe they are having him on.

Suddenly Paul appears from the back of the service area.

'Thought you were hiding from Jonathan and his car,' I chip in.

'Nope, let's have a look,'

They all troop out to the car, and listen to the noisy exhaust.

'Probably best thing I can do is to take off the loose pipe, but I've got to tell you if it is to do with the catalytic converter, they could be an arm and a leg,' Paul said.

'That sounds very expensive,' said Jonathan looking forlorn.

'I think I'll get a newspaper, and see you round the corner in the pub,' I said walking off.

I go into the shop, have to wait quite some time to get myself a paper, with the local mums, their kids and a few 'hoddies' delaying my progress. I then go into the sixteenth century pub next door, which had once been a staging inn. There are three or four old boys and a couple, in the lounge bar which has a huge open fire place, just right for banqueting in Henry Vlll's time and my time.

'There's a bloke looking for you,' piped up one of the locals.

'What a small bloke, going bald, cheeky chappie?'

'That's him,' chimed in an old guy with not many teeth.

I approach the bar, nod to a tall young bar maid wearing a broach with the name Emily written on it.

'Two Guinness please, back shortly...' I left my newspaper on the bar, and disappeared through a fire exit door at the front of the pub.

I wonder down the road towards a much seedier looking pub, which is probably older than the one I have just been in, definitely the poor relation, just the place for Richard lll. I spy Jonathan just leaving it.

'Oi, Jonathan, you twat, that's the wrong pub, bit grubby isn't it? Diana won't go in there.'

'Oh, I don't know, thought it was alright.'

They head back to the first pub, and duck back through the fire exit door.

'Oh, you found him then,' the toothless one said.

'Wondering the streets no less.'

'I bet.'

I go to the bar again where Emily has just poured the second Guinness.

'This is my 'dad', Jonathan, and I am Chris! Haven't been in here for ages Jonathan.'

'It is a beautiful building, glorious architecture and mouldings to die for,' says Jonathan wondering around the enormous bar area, whilst being tracked by the locals.

'I first came here when I was doing a bit of filming, before I had moved up here, came down from London for the day, a good news story sort of thing for the Foreign Office, with some sort of BBC producer. The crew brought me in here for lunch on a cold day, huge roaring log fire, didn't want to leave. Now look what's happened. I live up here.'

'That's your fault then Chris, you want to try Battersea on a Saturday morning, traffic jams everywhere and generally a bloody din going on.'

'Sure, but I thought you liked urban living. Let me get this.'

Chris gets out a twenty pound note, puts in on the bar. Jonathan intervenes says he is paying.

'And a packet of crisps as it is Saturday,' Chris said as passes a Guinness to Jonathan.

'That'll be eight pounds ten pee,' Emily the bar maid sad quietly.

'Blimey, that's expensive, that's why I never go to pubs Chris.'

'You mean, you never buy any drinks, so you wouldn't know the price Jonathan.'

Everyone is listening and watching Jonathan and myself clowning around, adding their own odd cryptic comment. I start to chat with Emily.

'You from round here? I'm originally from London'

'Yes I'm from Diss,' said Emily smiling.

'Are you studying or working elsewhere?'

'Well, I'm just finishing my gap year before I go to university to read classics.'

'Amazing, my son Daniel read classics at Edinburgh University.'

'Oh.'

'He did classics at school, then started at college, gave it up and went onto to do languages. Speaks Spanish, French and Portuguese fluently. Broker in New York now, poor sod.'

'Really.'

'How's your Latin Emily?' I enquired.

'Well, I am going learn Latin at University, we only studied classical civilization at A level at Diss High School, but I did languages French and Spanish too.'

'Y durante cuantos anos has estudado la lengua Espanola?' I chip in with my ancient Castillian style Spanish. (How many years did you study Spanish for ?)

'Poco, poco anos,' Emily mumbled.

'Small world, I did some part-time Sociology A level teaching at your school. I used to be a lecturer before I went into the film and television business via the Royal College of Art. Your school was a great school for Humanities, and the study of classics is a dying art now. You are one of the few to study Greek and Latin.'

'I know I was lucky.'

'The school was led by a great man, Peter Hiscocks, when I was there a couple of years ago.'

'Oh, I was there then,' Emily smiled.

'Must have passed each other in the corridor,' I said drinking up my pint.

'Well let me tell you a thing or two about art college Emily,' Jonathan said, butting in.

With that a wizened oldish looking bloke across the bar, wearing a Maoist type cap, with a goatee beard, a small gold earring and a roll-up behind his left ear, pipes up from across the other side of the long bar.

'I was an art teacher for many years, ended up head of the art department down the road in Weyton.'

Jonathan leaps up.

'Oh, hi, I'm Jonathan and this is my mate Chris, we're both at the Royal College of Art, different Departments though.'

'I'm Brett Pattison, I just bought myself a half a million pound house down the road, with workshops and I have even got a kiln,' said old goatee.

'No showing off now,' I said.

'Well, I used to love teaching art to these kids and even adults. They would often say they wished they had started art years ago. Some of the kids when they had left school, no matter what they were doing, even if they worked on the roads, would turn up to my local exhibitions. They would often chose a picture, say they could not pay for it, could they pay on the drip. Sure I used to say, pound a week and that's how it was.'

'Hold on, I'll come over there,' I said.

'Where are you off to now Chris?' asked Jonathan.

'Trade secrets, and what about another?'

'Bloody alcoholic….get it yourself!'

I go round to the other side of the bar where Brett is standing with a Guinness. I notice a copy of The Times newspaper. I had snobbishly assumed from the other side of the bar that this art teacher Brett would read more of a newspaper rag, like The Sun, rather than a so called quality paper, like the Times.

'Well? So you were an art teacher and then head of department. In my day the art department was always some sort of haven, rather like the music department,' I suggested.

'There were only a few good teachers really. Most of them were rather mealy mouthed and always complaining about their mortgages.'

'The bohemian art teacher, rebel without a cause and all that. But were you a practicing artist as well, before teaching ?' I asked.

'Of course, fine art, sculpture, pottery, carving you name it,' stated Brett.

'Amazing, where did you train ?'

'Went to the Ruskin College in Oxford years ago.'

'Film and Television School at Royal College of Art, myself.'

Jonathan shouts across the bar at me.

'Are we having a drink or what Chris?'

'Hold on Jonathan, Brett went to Ruskin College.'

'So what?'

Jonathan starts to chat to Emily who seems to be amused by our banter.

I turn back to Brett.

'So how did you survive in teaching so long? I gave up teaching after a few years, and went into the film business, after graduating at the RCA. But I suppose you have got a good pension. Seems to be the best thing to have these days,' I enquired.

'Yup,' said Brett looking a little sheepish.

'Well after I left teaching, and went into the film industry, I directed and produced mostly television commercials to pay the mortgage. Thought I had sold myself to the devil, Mephistopheles, and all that. Tried writing feature film scripts, but getting them made is like trying to find gold. What about you Brett?'

'I found it difficult as a teacher when I was working in Kent, and I looked around for other things to do after school. I did a lot of pub sign writing, used to get £500 a pop,' Brett said.

'Nice little earner, I used to paint and decorate properties. Still do.'

'Then some people from London approached me about some reproduction work,' continued Brett.

'Like for art dealers or those poster and print shops that were around in the eighties?' I quizzed Brett gently.

'Yes, that sort of thing. I mean at one time I was getting one thousand pounds a month as a teacher, and five thousand pounds doing copies for these guys,' Brett said quietly.

'Wow quite a difference. You mean copies for rich clients like Americans then. I suppose it would be Arabs and Chinese these days.'

'I don't know who they were for. I used to meet these art lot from London up in Ipswich and we just sort of went from there.'

'I mean I have just taken up painting in the long winter hours. I am doing copies from artists like Paul Klee, Mondrian, Picasso and Erte, just sort of finding my way. Not that difficult. A very heavy graphic style, I am enjoying it immensely. Should have got started years ago. But they are just freely adapted copies. Were you into serious copies, sort of art forgery then?'

'It was copies, 'in secundis',' Brett said looking across the bar.

' 'In secundis', what does that mean exactly, I know it means 'second' from my limited school Latin. But ?'

'Well, it means you sign it on the back of the painting, writing 'in secundis', then they know where you are coming from.'

'Rather like the a provenance of a painting……It is amazing at art sales and auctions, especially in the global market. I was in London the other day and went down Duke Street opposite the Royal Academy and ended up in Chrisite's Auction Rooms where they were selling minor works of Monet, Manet, George Grosz and even a small Picasso.'

'And what did you find?'

'Basically, all seemed well in the art world. Certainly plenty of money changing hands, no shortage of funds there.'

'I used to enjoy it,' sighed Brett.

'Different to teaching. What happened, why don't you do them now, you are not too old ?'

'Things changed. There are still thousands of copies out there, some experts reckon up to forty per cent of the art market,' Brett stated.

'So you were asked not to make any more copies, sort of nicked?'

'I painted a Modigliani copy. Then an expert at Sothebys, somehow got my telephone number and called me, and seriously quizzed me. Then I thought it was time to pack it in.'

'I hope you had not signed it as well, just the 'in secundis' on the back of the picture.'

'It was complicated.'

'Another pint,' I asked.

'No, no, I mustn't. I have been stopped by the police a couple of times for being over the limit.'

'Nasty business, police. Anyway come and meet my mate Jonathan.'

Brett and I move back across the bar to where Jonathan is chatting up Emily.

'Jonathan this is Brett. He is an artist, now lives up here, away from London. Just like you want to do, you silly old fart.'

'Hi, Jonathan I would buy you a drink but I have to go now. I got to watch it with the police. See yer.' Brett said quickly. He turns down a long dark wooden paneled corridor, and heads out towards the car park.

'Who the fuck was that old tosser, he seemed to know it all ?' demanded Jonathan.

'That my son, was an art forger. Hid behind the cloak of saying he was doing seconds of main stream artists. I think he actually signed a copy of a Modigliani that he had done, and then Sothebys came looking. Probably been inside, by the look of him.'

'Really. Anyway my motor should be ready now. Do you want to walk back with me to the garage see if it is OK, expect they have just cut that loose bit off the exhaust pipe?'

'Bye Emily, and thanks very much, hope Jonathan wasn't a nuisance. Good luck with your studies, especially the Latin and Greek,' I said.

'Bye, bye for now. Lovely pub,' Jonathan said, waving to the rest of the people in the bar.

Jonathan and I leave the pub and start walking round to the garage.

'That Emily, was a lovely girl. Quite posh too. It must have been a decent school the one she was at. Said she was half Italian, her mother was Italian and that her Dad went to Sandhurst. Lovely long legs and body to match. Go well at my life drawing classes at the Royal Academy on Mondays nights,' Jonathan declared.

'You still going to that stuff, all that flesh!'

We walk past Jonathan's car which is in the street now. Inside the small Korean car there is a large piece of exhaust pipe on the back seat.

'Right, that looks fixed!' Jonathan said.

'Yes, thinking about it, Emily was rather elegant, could be good for a Modigliani model or a least a copy of one, if you get my drift.'

'Whatever. Suppose this will cost me, I hate garages.'

'See you back at the ranch, time for some lunch.'

Over The Top

One of the worst things in life is pitching an idea which needs financial backing. How far does one go, and when do you start in, at say a restaurant meeting. Do you have a pleasant lunch and leave the pitch to the end? With everyone being so busy these days and mobile phones ruling people's lives this is perhaps a risky venture. But if you start your pitch at the beginning of the lunch, perhaps giving the impression that once business is over everyone can relax, the other party might think that you are in too much of a hurry to be taken seriously.

When one has a powerful idea or scheme for making money, but does not have the backing, there is a possible compunction to mention this idea at social occasions such as parties, dinners and other chance interactions, as well as formal planned occasions. Overdo it possibly!

People who are involved in start-up companies often seem to be a little pre-possessed, not being able to talk about anything else.

Film and television production of good ideas and stories comes high on that list of the never ending quest for financial backing. Producers and directors always have films in development which really means that they are looking for financial backing, plus securing a great cast and a viable film script, and trying to sell the package to a sales agent or distributor.

I happened to be in this situation myself, trying to raise money for an art house movie, based on a story by a well-known English novelist. 'The package' consisted of a top Hollywood director, top casting and a very successful British producer. The trouble was nobody seemed to be able to raise the money for this production. I offered my services with a view to gaining an introductory fee, and a possible percentage point or part-point, on gross profits if there were any. There often aren't.

It was a medieval Christian story. Most of these Christian films make serious money as there seems to be a very big worldwide market for them with over two billion Christians out there globally. I was brought up as a Catholic and thought that this might be the way forward, knowing what I knew, so to speak.

At various meetings with the Director and the Producer, I was told not to flood the market place with requests for money, not to flog the project around town. Otherwise it would lose credibility. My agent even told me to be quiet and listen at these meetings and not to tell jokes. No fun.

So I approached my network of contacts with caution, only approaching one banker I knew socially, and an old school friend who was a Catholic and now in the House of Lords. The trouble was the world seemed to be in global meltdown financially with banks going bust and governments shoring up the Western banking system. Film financing was not high on their list.

At a quiet luncheon in the centre of London, the banker friend told me he had lost all his money bar ten per cent, and he was now out of a job as his bank had gone bust. I felt that I should be helping him out.

My contact in the House of Lords whom I thought would have lots of financial contacts, said it was like a 'nuclear winter' out there financially, and not to bother. Well OK! Even so I was after my fee.

I kept pursuing the possibility of raising this finance. At a meeting with another private banker whom I had been introduced to in my London media club, I was told that the Producer had already shown him the film project, and that he would be delighted to handle the film finances once we had raised them elsewhere!

My first banker friend sent me an email suggesting that I contact a guy in a very slick media funding company which looked after footballers and other sports personalities, and very affluent business people who used film and television productions as a tax vehicle to lower their exposure to the UK tax system. All legit, plus a good investment in a successful film netted them a good return. This funding company had had many such successes on major feature films.

A grand meeting was set up with this media company, and held in their Soho offices in central London. One of their very bright Oxford graduates, ex-Goldman Sachs, asked the Director to outline the story.
I was asked to outline the potential market and distribution, and the Producer handed over a glowing cast list. The script had been fully developed and written.

Emails went round after this meeting, there was good potential here, if we could introduce a rich individual or as they say ' a high net worth individual', then they could work out the best tax vehicle for the financing of this picture.

My lawyer was always going on about a rich Anglo-Arab guy he knew. A meeting was set up in a gastro pub in Mayfair. I arrived early with a presentation document, looked around the bar, saw an Arab looking guy downing double vodkas and guessed that was my man. My lawyer arrived and introductions were made.

After more drinks, this guy called a hedge fund financier, who spoke to me directly via speaker phone. He said he was interested and would I send over the document. He sounded as if he was speaking from the bottom of a bucket. Afterwards I did some chasing mainly be email, but never heard from them again.

Shortly after I went to New York to see my son who had gone to work there as a stockbroker. He introduced me to one of his associates who said he might be interested in backing this film. Dinner at a fashionable Italian restaurant was arranged in Manhattan with the Director. The two of them seemed to get onto together. More emails and no replies.

Back in England I reviewed my strategy. It seemed fairly hopeless, but I was convinced this film would make money because of the potential in-built Christian audience. Bums on seats, the seats were almost sold already! An American film about Jesus Christ had recently been made on a lowish budget, less than USD $25 million, even with sub-titles and not that good a film really, but had made over half a billion dollars in gross profits worldwide. So there was a precedent, and our budget was less, at around USD $15 million. I thought I might as well press on.

I had further connections too, being a partner in a film company in Melbourne, Australia. My two partners were very successful commercial lawyers, one of whom had worked as a film packaging lawyer in a successful film company in Melbourne, the other as the Finance Director for Rio Tinto Zinc in Japan. Heavy hitters.

We had a number of projects in development or 'on the slate'. It looked as if we were going to be aligned with a very wealthy Australian business man who wanted to start an Australian film foundation. Plus the lead singer of an immensely successful Australian rock band wanted to put a couple of million into one of our musical film projects.
So there was potential for film funding there. My two partners had already met the Director of this medieval religious film, at a play our company had commissioned and produced in Melbourne. At the time, the Director had been doing some digital editing there for his latest feature film.

When I strongly suggested that our company should become involved with the financing of this Christian project, it was quietly put to one side, inspite of the potential of tying it in with some senior Australian actors. Oh well.

So I happened to be at a post-Christmas luncheon party at a house in the country which was owned by my banker friend who had lost most of his money in the financial global melt-down, but not the house.

There, I met a husband and wife with their two young children. In the conservatory I got chatting with the youngish husband, over a couple of drinks.

He said he was a Commissioning Editor at a British television company. A friend of a friend. In fact the brother-in-law. I talked about my work in the film industry, and he talked about how much money a friend of his was making shooting film commercials all over the world. He seemed to be interested in making more money, than he was currently earning in his television company.

So the I launched into a pitch about this Christian medieval film. It was quite impassioned, I told the story, talked about the budget, the potential for massive gross profits, the comparison with another low budget British film about a past King's speech impediment, and the glorious cast list of course.

When I had finished this informal but passionate pitch, the husband looked directly at me and said meekly,

'Sorry but, I am only in TV documentaries, like another drink?'

Antiques

Piers was at an antique auction in a market town in South Norfolk, when he decided to check through the catalogue for any potential bargains that he might have missed when he viewed the items the day before. He sat down at an antique desk in the middle of the auction room, and thumbed through the catalogue. All seemed much the same as yesterday's viewing.

He looked around at the auction crowd whilst sipping his cappuccino.

'Same old grey haired crinklies,' he mumbled to himself.

He carefully put his coffee down on the desk in front of him. Piers then did a closer inspection of the desk he was sitting at. It was exactly the same type of desk, as the one his father had had in the dining room at their home in North London many moons ago. In the auction catalogue, Lot no.91, was described as:

'A "Cookes of Finsbury London" Georgian revival mahogany twin pedestal writing desk with tooled leather insert over eight drawers on a plinth base.' Guide price £380- £510

That sounded about right.

Piers's father had been a very successful antique dealer after the Second War in London's West End, in a shop off Baker Street, at No.39, George Street. His father had described it, as his 'gold-mine' on several occasions. Not always easy to find these gold nuggets, but they were there, if you looked.

As a youngster, Piers often used to come down on the bus to visit his father, who for a treat would take him for shepherd's pie or bangers and mash in the pub opposite. Sometimes when Piers arrived at the shop, there was a hand written sign up in the window, saying 'back in one minute' or worse 'back in five minutes' which always seemed like an eternity. His father was out seeing clients, or round at the Wallace Collection in Manchester Square seeking advice, or just admiring the Canalettos there.

Occasionally, Piers was asked do an errand and go round to Selfridges on Oxford Street. Quite an adventure for a ten year old boy in shorts. Selfridges seemed like a huge place, and in those days the store still had wires attached to the ceilings which carried over the cash in little steel boxes to the main cashier. To the young Piers this was great fun, possibly better than his Hornby Double 'O O' train set at home. His father told Piers that if there was any problem, say to the person:

'You are the son of your father.'

His shop had one of those bells with a spring on the top of the door which rang when you opened it. The floor joists were old & shaky and the whole shop seemed to wobble as you crossed over to the back of the shop. It was pretty terrifying for the eight year old Piers in his short trousers and khaki shirt. All the antiques seem to tremble at once. It was a great relief to get to the back of the shop where there was an alcove with an armchair on the left, a kind of refuge point. His father used to sit at his desk at the back, looking out over the shop for any potential customers. Above him the ceiling plaster had fallen down leaving a big patch with bare lathes.

The shop looked rather chaotic, especially at the back with piles of stuff heaped up, plus smaller antiques balanced precariously on various shelves. It looked like you might find a bargain, possibly an expensive antique which the owner might not necessarily be aware of.

However, Piers' father knew exactly what most of his stock was worth. On every piece there was a self-adhesive label with a brief description and his secret code which indicated what price he had paid and what he might sell the piece for. No item had a clear price tag on it for the public. Pier's eldest brother knew the code, but it was rather complicated for Piers to understand as a child.

His father was well known in the West End, and some other dealers gave him their stock on a sale or return basis. There were deals to be done, a sort of 'gentlemanly haggling.'

Downstairs there was a large damp and dark basement filled with stock in old brown boxes, some of them definitely looked pre-War. A hidden gold mine. On the half landing was a rather disgusting looking toilet. Outside on the little landing was a small gas ring which Piers' father used to boil eggs on for his Spartan lunches. It was cold and miserable in the winter months, with just a single bar electric fire, heating the back of the shop.

This was the mid-fifties, the War and food rationing were not long gone.
Out of all this, his father Anthony had managed to send his four sons to Catholic private school or what the English called 'public schools', in the 1950's with the income he produced from his 'gold-mine'.

At boarding school in a history class one of the priests used to teach, the priest had suggested that all antique dealers were sharks except of course Piers' father.

To this day Piers could not comprehend how his father had done it. When Piers had paid for one of his own children to go private day school twenty five years later, it had nearly bankrupted him

In his house, Piers still kept a black and white photograph of his father proudly standing at the front of his shop surrounded by his antiques, and dressed smartly in his usual three piece suit, ready for business.

The antique desk that they had at home had always seemed very important to Piers' father, and his four sons were told not to touch it. As a child Piers only touched the desk when his father was not there. To him it was not full of antiques, more full of junk. In the left hand drawers there were old paper clips, bits of string, sealing wax and lots of stuff, including old letters and post cards. The right hand ones seemed to hold more papers with lots of figures on them, probably outline valuations for customers, old cheque books, occasional pieces of glass jewellery, even the odd cough sweet, half used tubes of glue, more bits of string, and the odd glass coloured paper weight. But it always seemed fun to open these drawers, secretly go through them, and see what they held.

So Piers found himself sitting in front of a similiar desk in the spring of 2011. In fifty years the antique markets seemed to have changed radically.

Piers often heard the well-worn clichés from dealers.

'There's no market for this sort of stuff anymore' or 'The market's not there anymore'

Piers wasn't convinced. In London at a major auction houses such as Christies or Sotheby's the market for fine antiques, furniture and fine art seemed to be very alive and well. There seemed to be a rarified financial atmosphere that was recession proof.
Piers thought that perhaps your average middle class household no longer had an antique plate or vase in the pride of place at home. More people seemed to

like the new wave of restored vintage furniture together with other newer nick-nacks. Even the 1950's retro style was commanding big prices. The gothic style seemed to be expanding rapidly too. It just reminded Piers of horror films, and sub-cultures, tastes and styles that he no longer understood or liked particularly.

Towards the end of his successful career in antiques in the West End, Piers' father Anthony had said that he was not going to re-new the shop lease, and would be moving out. At this time Piers was living in Islington in north London during the late 1970's, and not doing very well as a free-lance film director. Piers said that the Islington antique market seemed to be booming and maybe his father would like to take a smaller, less expensive shop there.

Islington at the time had a mixed reputation socially, with many new comers such as judges, actors, musicians and city people piling into its streets of dilapidated Georgian houses which were snapped up and renovated.

But behind this new middle class façade the Cockney tribe still seemed to be ruling the roost. Piers's father was not so sure about making a commitment to a new shop lease there, but suggested that maybe Piers should hire one of the Saturday stalls and see how he did at selling some of his less expensive antiques.

Having put together a number of antique pieces, Piers's father then priced them, and boxed them up with Piers. Piers had to take a downstairs stall at the Islington antique market . That was Piers's first mistake. The downstairs market seemed to be absolutely dead. The other stall holders seemed to consist of a number of fade away actresses who were between acting parts, and a few grumpy old poofs with dyed hair. Never mind that there were no customers. All the passing trade was hanging around the market stalls outside or in the shops upstairs.

Also Piers thought that his father had over-priced the items that he had selected. Piers could not stand the hanging around, just waiting for potential customers. Piers thought that his father had done this for a good part of his life in his shop. Even in the West End of London, there were times when he did not make a sale for a couple of weeks. It was all very gloomy at home, till the cloud lifted and antiques were sold again.

His father had once asked Piers if he wanted to come into the antique business with him. Piers had declined saying it was not busy enough for him. Piers opted for a glamorous career in film with acres of down time and insecurity instead, plus hanging around between shots on the set!

At around 5pm, Piers's father turned up in his three piece suit, he had been to work on a Saturday too, and asked Piers how it had gone.

'Not well Dad, I think it is too quiet down here, the stalls upstairs seem to be getting all the passing trade, but there is a waiting list for them. Didn't take a penny.'

'Want some tea and a piece of cake? Then let's call it a day.'

'Thanks Dad.'

Piers' father eventually decided to move his shop from the West End to a larger more suburban shop up the Finchley Road in North West London, to be nearer home. After the working day Piers used to come to the shop in the West End and pack up stock and drive it over in his small Mini Traveller, to the new premises for his father. This became a kind of pilgrimage, and Piers was glad when the move was done.

Time passed and Piers used to visit his father up there in his new premises. He was now some seventy years old. They would go out to have shepherd's pie and a beer in the pub up the road, or the occasional curry in the restaurant opposite.

Quite often when Piers sat in this shop, his father used to nod off to sleep. He had managed to create a sitting space, hidden by a little screen, at the back of the shop similar to the one he had in the West End. He still seemed to be in control, with a back pocket full of money, often in different currencies, many customers, different bank accounts and carrying out numerous valuations for many of his ageing clients who lived round about. Long working days, every day except Sunday.

At that time during the late 1970's, Piers tried to be a la mode and had quite long hair with sideburns to match. More often than not, when Piers visited his father in the shop, as Piers was leaving his father would get up and say

'I'll give you five pounds if you get your hair cut.'

'No Dad it's OK. I like it the way it is.'

'Sure?'

'Sure Dad, thanks.'

Piers was in his early thirties now, with a divorce pending.

Over the next few years his father started to gradually wind things down, and there was talk about him maybe closing the shop, and what would happen to all his substantial stock of antiques.

During this time, Piers took a job in Nairobi, Kenya for two years, running a film production company directing and producing cinema commercials which were post-produced in London. Thought he needed a break after his divorce.

Piers got back at the end of July, via Khartoum and Sudan Airways, which he called 'Shake, Rattle & Roll'

Airlines, after his Kenyan contract had finished. He had decided he did not like being a big fish in a small pond in Nairobi, plus his father was due for a second cataract operation. He already seemed to have had a very slight stroke down one side, from the previous operation, as he kept squeezing a rubber ball in his right hand, attempting to get full feeling back in his hand.

On the day before the operation, Piers drove his mother and father to St. Thomas' Hospital. They argued non-stop all the way there. Piers remembered one of the reasons he had gone to Kenya in the first place, and wondered why he had come home. The night before his father had his operation Piers visited him. He seemed to be quite lively. He looked quite dapper in his silk dressing gown as he walked Piers to the lift after his visit. At that time cataract operations were done under full anesthetic.

The next day was Saturday, and Piers's mother phoned him in Islington in the late morning.

'I think we better go to the hospital. The matron has just phoned. I better bring him some new pyjamas.'

'Why what has happened Mum ?'

'Probably had some mishap, Piers.'

'Doesn't sound like it. I'll be right over.'

When Piers saw his Dad in the hospital bed, he thought he was dead. His mother thought he was just asleep after the operation. The surgeon and matron made the appropriate overtures and explained that Piers's father had suffered a major stroke and was paralysed all down his right hand side.

It was all a major shock for the family. As reality sank in Piers and his elder brothers talked about what should be done with the shop and all the stock of antiques. It was agreed that the shop lease should be given up and the stock brought back to the family house and put in the large triple garage. Initially some of the finer antiques were placed in a pucker West End auction house just off Bond Street. This was done by Piers's older brothers.

A few weeks later, at another family meeting the brothers went through the auction results. Piers was amazed to find that very low reserves had been placed on some of the best pieces, including Meissen, Spode, Worcester, Wedgwood and Royal Doulton antiques, some valuable Chinese vases, plates and some Japanese miniature ivory carvings.

'This is crazy, I am going down to sort these reserve prices out. If we can't get the right prices there, we would be better off selling them bit by bit in Islington market,' said Piers forcibly to his brothers.

They nodded at him, indicating that he should get on with it.

Piers re-jigged all the reserves on the remaining pieces and secured a much better result for his father's auctioned antiques. This was important as this was the main income for their mother, who still had some expensive tastes, including occasional visits to the Harrods store.

Piers suggested that they ought to try the antique markets in Islington. He would try to book one of the stalls upstairs. His second brother Chris who was struggling financially wanted to help too. The idea was that they would try Saturday mornings and take a slice off the top of anything they sold, which they would split. This suited Piers as he was now unemployed again having just finished as a director on a short-term contract making small arts films for a regional television station.

Another flash in the pan.
So after a gap of ten years Piers found himself back at the antique market in Islington again. This time without his father.

Piers collected a selection of antiques in their old pre-war looking boxes from the family garage and packed them up in his bright yellow Ford Capri. His mother used to wind him up about his divorce whilst she cooked him a Welsh rarebit with an egg on the top. Then it was out of the house, into the loaded car with a Booker T tape blaring away, as Piers scudded back to Islington over the top of Hampstead Heath.

Once home he unpacked, and cleaned the antiques and then re-packed again them into the brown boxes with their old newspaper. The day started early, and the stalls were being prepared from 6 am onwards, mainly with trade customers hovering around like vultures.

Piers and his brother became an overnight success in the antiques market. The trade vultures had not seen them in the market before, and when they started unpacking these pre-war style boxes they nearly went berserk trying to outbid each other. Piers and Chris played on this.

'Piers should I sell this for fifty pounds, what do you think?'

'Chris that's far too cheap and you know it is. Got to be eighty'

The trade punter would then come in at sixty and then be out bid by someone else at seventy. Result or what!

At around 9am they had already often taken over one thousand pounds, time for a bacon buttery, tea and coffee and to see how the other stall holders were doing.

Nothing seemed to stop Piers and his brother Chris. One day they got the works of a very old clock out of one of these boxes. The market seemed to go quiet, a rumour went round that something seriously valuable had come up. Some of the senior dealers and antique shop owners started hovering. It was late November, the price went up and up. Piers keep saying

'Chris we can't sell that, let's withdraw it and get it valued by a museum.'

Although his brother Chris was an engineer, and could repair clocks Piers was not actually sure his brother knew the real value of this clock, which appeared to be made up of very thin wooden parts and a tiny mechanism, rather post medieval looking. This all helped to bring further tension to the market atmosphere. Then the fifty pound notes started coming across. It was their best sale as street traders in the market, and made their mother a few thousand pounds.

Often they would be finished by 12 noon on a Saturday, having sold just about everything, packed up the stall, loaded up the car, and then managed to sell the stall on to someone for the continuing afternoon trade. So the pitch had cost nothing.

Then it was back to Piers little house in the rougher end of Islington off the Caledonian Road, go through the receipt book, unload the money, separate it into fifties, twenties, tens, fivers and coins. Count it all up, take their slice and put the majority of the money into an envelope to take back to Piers's mother, the following week. It was never less than a thousand pounds.

Piers and Chris meet other stall holders, one of whom was a struggling barrister, and another who had a small wine business in Wapping in East London. The great thing about this wine merchant was that he had some cheap wine that he sold off at one pound a bottle. Often the first port of call was to get a few cases of red and white loaded up as well. Then it was round to the pub in Barnsbury to recount all the stories of how sales were achieved in the morning.

This was one of the first times Piers seemed to be flush with cash, that he could buy a few drinks and afford maybe some beef for Sunday lunch. It was certainly the first time that he had seen and handled the new fifty pound notes that come into circulation at the end of the seventies.

Over the next nine months, Piers and Chris became well known in the antique market, but started to lose some of their initial sales fervour as the traders and shop keepers got used to their selling antics.

But on one memorable occasion when they had kicked off at 6am, there were traders out bidding each other and a small Scotsman, called Alan, thought he had secured a deal with Piers, when suddenly a huge cockney dealer had him round the neck suggesting that it was his antique, not Alan's.

That was how hot their antique market stall got at times. Piers had done a double take at his brother when this happened. Afterwards Piers thought his father would have been proud of him.

But it was miles away from the polite buying and selling in his father's West End shop. At one time his father had counted three ex-kings of Europe as his clients. In the Islington antique market there seemed to be only Cockney barons.

Like all good things this antique market life came to an end. At times it had been very hard especially standing out in the winter and with the rain coming down and everything getting soggy.

It had bonded Piers and his brother Chris and tied them over financially in a small way. Piers was now a free-lance director in Soho on commercials and lower budget features films. It sounded good, but often meant unemployment. Chris was struggling with three young children in private school. But overall they had shifted their father's antique stock, and made their mother over forty thousand pounds which increased her number of visits to Harrods store somewhat.

Four years later Piers father died at home in the drawing room next to a cabinet full of antiques and the family house had to be cleared as it had been sold. In order to clear it two large skips were hired and placed on the drive. Most of the stuff came from the triple garage where all the remaining antiques had been stored.

There were vast numbers of valuation documents, all wrapped up in old copies of the Daily Telegraph which acted as Piers's father sort of briefcase. In amongst these documents, pieces of papers with codes and prices, were various amounts of money in different currencies, as his father would accept foreign currencies to make a sale easier. If foreign clients went away to change their money into pounds they often never came back.

There was also many esoteric bottles of booz which Piers and his brother Chris helped themselves to whilst sorting through and clearing this accumulation of stuff into the skips outside.

Piers thought that his other three brothers should be more careful about going through these papers. He was convinced that there was money tucked away in all these old valuation papers. So he climbed into one of the skips and started going through the papers again. His brothers had all gone off to lunch. He was going to follow on.

After ten minutes of searching Piers came across a hoard of money in different denominations, amounting to over several hundred pounds. Piers knew that there was probably more, but it was a very sad time, now that his father was dead and they were selling the family home. So he left it.

Piers moved from Islington to West Hampstead and got re-married and become a successful film commercials director. But he always keep an eye open for antiques, and did have another go at selling antiques in the Islington market but like everything else it had changed.

There did not seem to be the demand. Plus he had to buy the stock in now. It was a different world.

However, when Piers had to get one of his Apple Mac computers repaired, he went up to a repair depot in Hendon, North West London. He was meet by the manager who was from Norway. He asked Piers if he was related to an antiques dealer he had known in the West End who had the same surname as Piers. Piers replied that he was his youngest son. The IT Norwegian guy said that Piers father had given him a good bit of advice,

'Always travel with an antique.'

He had always done this and made quite a lot of money in America as a result. Piers told the Norwegian guy that the other advice his father often told people was,

'An antique is the best investment.'

The years rolled by and at the end of July 2001 Piers moved up to south Norfolk, after renovating a property in Belsize Park, a rich suburb of North London, as most of his film work had dried up. Then 9/11 hit and the world seemed to go crazy.

Piers inherited a few of his father's antiques that he had kept in a cabinet in the dining room at home. There was a Chinese Green dragon, an Art Deco ivory dancer, called 'Belle de Jour' and some Staffordshire figures. Plus his second wife Victoria who was the daughter of a chemist had inherited some Masons Ironstones jugs plus some valuable pharmacy jars. These now resided in a cabinet in the drawing room in their fine Georgian rectory in the country.

After about nine months after moving in, Piers had the windows cleaned. Shortly afterwards they were robbed. The sash window had been forced, but nothing much was taken except one suitcase and all the antiques. It looked like it was robbery to order. The police came, and were as helpful as they could be. A case number was given, but the antiques were not recovered. So an insurance claim was put in.

Piers was told by the insurers to replace the Masons Ironstone, and pharmacy jars at auction, and to let them know what the cost was. He thought this was absurd as how could you tell what price you would pay at auction. So he went to London to a shop in Church Street Kensington, which specialized in Mason's Ironstone and got some realistic replacement prices.

Eventually a list of the missing items and estimated valuations was got up and sent to the insurance company.

Piers made a call from the dining room where he was working on a film script, to the insurance company to see where they were on his claim. As he was waiting he glanced at an old picture of his father's on the mantelpiece. The picture showed a dealer in antiques talking to a wavering customer looking at an antique plate full of repairs and rivets holding it together.

The caption read:

'Half-a-crown too much for it! Why, there's sixteen bob's worth of rivets in it!'

Piers thought people would not even know what a rivet is today. Then the insurance broker came on the line, and tried to fob Piers off with a low settlement figure. After a discussion with his brother in law, Piers phoned back the insurance broker, said that he was not prepared to settle for the offered amount. Piers used the phrase 'estimated insurance replacement valuation' which his brother in law had suggested would get a better deal. The insurance broker asked if Piers would hold the line.

The broker came back in a couple of minutes and agreed to settle the claim in full, three times as much as the original offer.

Piers and his wife Victoria decided not to replace the antiques but had the back hall re-built as it was falling down. Piers argued against re-placement.

'What's the point of owning anything valuable, they only steal it these days?'

But Piers still missed some of the stolen antiques, especially the dancing ivory figure of 'Belle de Jour' and the somewhat gaudy Mason's Ironstone jugs which were owned by his wife.

So Piers was here at the auction in South Norfolk, catalogue in hand, sitting behind a desk similar to the one they had at home. He had come to buy a present for his wife. Item 81 was listed as:

'Four Mason's Ironstone jugs' guide price £35-£60.'

Piers thought this was rather cheap, having checked their authenticity out the day before. He started thinking that in the West End years ago they would have gone for much more.

Lot no.81 came up. Piers bid, so did three other people, plus a telephone bid. Up the price went. Piers felt under pressure. The London traders were there. £280 pounds secured the Mason's Ironstone for Piers who afterwards looked round the auction room to see who might have challenged him, ' the son of his father', and the Piers who had never wanted to go into antiques. It was all over in a couple of minutes.

Piers waited on to see what the 'Georgian revival mahogany twin pedestal writing desk' lot no.91 went for. It did not reach its reserve
price and was not sold.

Piers gave the desk a gentle pat, picked up his catalogue and walked out of the auction room to go to pay his £280 pounds for lot no.81.

Not In My Backyard

'Less Eligibity'

The Royal Commission on the Poor Law:
The 1832 Royal commission onto the Operation of the Poor Law in England was set up following the widespread destruction and machine breaking of the Swing Riots. The report was prepared by a commission of nine, including Nassau William Senior, and served by Edwin Chadwick as Secretary.

The Commission proposed the New Law be governed by two overwhelming principles:

- "less eligibility": that the pauper should have to enter a workhouse with conditions worse than that of the poorest 'free' labourer outside of the workhouse.
- The "workhouse test", that relief should only be available in the workhouse. The reformed workhouses were to be uninviting, so that

anyone capable of coping outside them would chose not to be in one.

Wikipedia.org/English Poor Laws

Nigel Johnson had always believed in the need for renewable energy. This was not just because the world was heating up, more because he reckoned the way the world was gobbling up every fossil fuel, and with an ever expanding global population all wanting to join the party, most fuels like oil and gas were destined to extinction.

Nigel lived in London, he turned on the gas central heating in the autumn and turned it off in the spring. If it was extra cold on a winter's day he would just hit the heating button on the timer clock and have an extra couple of hours. Never thought twice about it. Gas was still relatively cheap then. He had noticed a rise in the petrol prices, but as he lived in London, he did not use his car much, going mostly on the Tube, so it never really bothered him.

After all the hullabaloo about the lights going out and computers going down when the year 2000 approached and the new millennium came in, Nigel thought it was probably time to leave city life and London, and try to become self-sufficient. Burn his own chopped wood, grow his own vegetables, fresh organic eggs, and raise a few Gloucester Old Spot pigs must be the way forward.

As Nigel was preparing his exit from London over the coming year, renewable energy became a hot political topic worldwide. If governments in the West were not supporting the Cato agreement, and all it stood for, they would be condemning the future generation to an ever more polluted and hotter planet. 'Global Warming' became the new bible. Renewable energy would help solve the energy problem, plus producing a clean source of natural energy.

The 'green' vote became a huge vote catcher. Governments developed schemes to help these new inventive alternative energy producers and their schemes which were heavily subsidized and which in turn attracted investors such as hedge funds.

Gradually, it seemed to Nigel that everywhere you looked in the newspapers, television and radio, the internet, industry and agriculture, everything had gone green. It was definitely the new holy cow. If one disagreed with any green policy you were placed very close to the devil and considered ignorant and socially irresponsible.

Even a well-known American novelist who also wrote popular television series and feature film scripts, became anathema in the eyes of the popular green press because he had dared to write a thriller novel that questioned the authenticity of global warming. He had suggested in this novel that environmental scientists might fudge their figures in order to secure continuing large financial grants for their vital green research.

Nigel had been brought up in the suburbs in London after the war when everything seemed pretty scarce, including electricity, gas, petrol and food. His father had always gone round the house turning off the lights if his family had left them on unnecessarily. Nowadays, people all seemed to leave their lights on, had many IT gadgets left on charging overnight, and people never unplugged their television sets. Modern kitchens were now a glossy shrine to electricity and gas consumption. Car journeys had become much longer but much quicker, with only a pretence to saving fuel by having the odd over-priced electric car, and bigger engines with better mileage consumption per gallon.

Globally car expansion was out of control with China and India leading the way after the USA. People just expected to consume endless amounts of energy, do what they like energy wise. It was the Western way, and everybody worldwide wanted to join this so called better way of life.

When cornered about global warming and green energy, Nigel often used to just say:

'Well, we could start by turning our lights out when we do not need them on, and turning all mobiles phones, computers, and televisions off when we go to bed.'

At home Nigel practiced what he preached, and went around the house turning off the lights when not needed. In the winter in his old Suffolk rectory it was like living in a gothic horror movie house. His wife Pauline did the opposite and turned everything on. It was like playing out some electronic ping-pong game which his wife was good at.

Nigel and Pauline had moved to north Suffolk to enjoy the benefits of a quiet rustic life, including less industrial blight, noise, traffic pollution and ugly buildings. They were now surrounded by farming land rather than terraced houses. However, all land has a value, and all land according to economists must pay a rent in some form or other.

Thus the gorgeous, tranquil rustic land opposite their large detached Georgian house was unexpectedly subject to a planning application for the erection of seven huge 400feet/120 metre wind turbines, bigger than Big Ben outside the Houses of Parliament. This was about saving the planet with renewable green energy. If it happened to be in Nigel's back yard, 'too bad', came the cry from city folk, city investors, and the green camp.

This planning limbo went on for over six years with the local farmer and renewable energy company, being refused planning permission for seven wind turbines, re-applying for a wind monitoring mast only which was granted, then putting in a further re-application for five wind turbines through a different renewable energy company, Trans Energy Limited, which was turned down by the County Council again on grounds of conservation and protection of the environment.

A local opposition group was formed. Nigel felt this group, in its militant opposition to these wind turbines was even more serious and intimidating than the green energy people. Another holy cow, Nigel thought, no time for jokes, just more stress. This was serious stuff, it affected people's lives and health, the value of their properties, and the preservation of the English countryside. So what thought Nigel was, we are just 'Nimbys' one and all.

In the end there was an appeal against the Council's decision and a tribunal was set up with an independent chair person. Solicitors and barristers for both sides, and mountains of paperwork, including an Environmental Impact Assessment report, and hundreds of letters of objection from all the surrounding villages, all posted on the council's website.

The lady Inspector for the tribunal allowed members of the public to make statements during an allotted time period of ten minutes each during the appeal hearing. Some of these statements were very emotive, some about effects on health, some people said they going to move if the appeal was successful, some were semi-scientific, and also included was an appeal from the local Member of Parliament. Each side thought they were right. The vast majority of the people did not want these vast wind turbines overlooking their back gardens.

Throughout the appeal Nigel began to feel that these local people mattered for nothing in the scheme of things. During the ten day appeal, he began to have thoughts that he and the other residents were less eligible, had less real rights than anybody wanting to produce green energy at any cost.

It was not quite like being cast out into the workhouse, but Nigel felt that he was now something of a second class citizen, had less rights, less eligibility when he was faced with the green question and renewable energy, and his own objection to the proposed wind turbines spoiling his tranquility and shattering his rustic views, indeed his whole Arcadian idyll!

After about some twenty statements being read from the public on the eighth day of the appeal, Nigel was the last to speak that morning. Having been trained at film school and worked in the film industry, he thought he would make a statement about the exact visual impact these huge industrial wind turbines would have. Of course the renewable energy company said they would have a minimal visual impact on the environment and the local countryside.

Nigel then went up and sat in front of the audience and turned his microphone on and made his visualization statement to all present.

Below is a copy of part of Nigel's statement to the appeal tribunal. Before making his statement Nigel handed out copies of his statement together with the visualisations and enlarged pictures to the Appeal Inspector, the appellants and the defendants.

Statement: Nigel Johnson

" My name is Nigel Johnson and I live at Rectory House, Beshall, Suffolk, directly opposite the proposed industrial wind turbine development at Lower Victoria Farm. I came here ten years ago from the middle of London for a bit of peace and quiet.

In terms of credibility, I would offer the following credentials:
I am an Economics graduate of Durham University, with a post-graduate qualification from London University, and a Master's Degree from the Film & Television School of the Royal College of Art.

I have been a successful film and TV commercials director for over thirty years, both working for PLC's, such as Molinare in London, and running my companies. Amongst others I have directed and produced for clients such as Nationwide Building Society, Associated Newspapers, De Beers Diamonds, Barclays Bank PLC and the United Nations Environment Programme.

Visualisations and translation of storyboards have been very much part of my daily work.

Currently, I am a director of Treetops Productions Limited which is 'packaging' feature films here and in Australia. All of the above can be verified through my agent Jessica Blake of Blake and Associates.

This morning I would like to question the basis of the visualization and methodology, as laid out in Trans Engergy's Environmental Impact Assessment Document. The visual impact of a 120 metre high wind turbine is a critical part of any decision making in the planning process. These observations would not only apply to this wind farm planning application, but also to other pending throughout the UK.

In my attempt to explain what I consider to be VALID visualization,
I will quote briefly from two letters of objection that I sent to the Planning Officer at Suffolk Council which were also sent to the Appeal Tribunal at Bristol. I will also reference professional journals as the 'Visualisation Standards' written by The Highland Council, and an Architects/Town Planning Visualisation guide.

In my second letter of objection sent to the Planning Services at Suffolk council 28th. October 2010, I questioned again Trans Energy's Environmental Impact Document and its poor visualisations standards used in its photography. I wrote:

"One of the first things you learn about in basic photography and film-making is how to *capture an image as it really is.* For this you use a single shot 35mm camera with a fixed 50mm lens. No if or buts. You do not join shots together, nor do you shoot from high up or below the image that you are trying to capture. You shoot on a level plain for true representation."

None of the above seems to have been carried out by Trans Energy's best practice methodology for attempting to visually represent how big these huge wind turbines would actually be. To summarise: Trans Energy's visualization have **not used standard 50mm representation.** They have used different lenses to suit their purposes, i.e. to minimize the visualization of the impact of these huge wind turbines."

Most people have heard of Zoom lenses, you can make distant objects bigger or smaller depending on what you want to do with the image. Just so with the use of a 28mm lens, which is known as a wide angle lens. This spreads and flattens the image, so that prominent objects in the foreground appear less prominent, and very large objects such as wind turbines on a flat scene fade back in the panorama or appear much smaller than they actually are. The 28mm lens is used in advertising, promotions, and often by estate agents. It is akin to the basic web camera, spreading the image, and distorting true representation of this image.

In an earlier letter sent to the Planning Services of Suffolk Council on 31st. March 2010, objecting to this planning application, I had identified in the Environmental Impact Assessment Document: Appendix 7.3 Photomontage Methodology that:

"A fixed 28mm lens was used in digital SLR format.."

I have <u>attached</u> the appropriate pages taken from Appendix 7.3 of the EIA.

In last week's presentation by so-called <u>expert witnesses</u>, during the Tribunal hearing I asked Mr. Benton, one of Trans Energy's expert witnesses on Environmental Impact, on Thursday 16th. June<u>, what lens was used in their visualization photography.</u>

I was told categorically by Mr. Benton that and I quote:

<u>**"A 50mm lens was used..."**</u>

I am afraid this does not add up. If the visualisations were created using a 28mm lens as outlined in Appendix 7.3 of the EIA, they cannot then be converted to a 50mm image.

They give completely different visual results. It would seem to me that a 28mm was used for the EIA to minimize the visual impact of the wind turbines, and then Trans Energy tried to gloss over this by having one of their expert witnesses, Mr. Benton, say it was a 50mm lens.

This an attempt to confuse the public into thinking that a 120 metre high wind turbine overlooking your back garden will hardly be seen! I mean they are doing this to create green energy and save the planet.

At this stage I will not go down the path of greedy profiteering new energy companies snapping up the 25 year government subsidies available for these schemes. However, to further quote from my letter:

"The developers claim that the image has been taken with a standard 50mm lens. but what they do not make clear is the fact that the full frame A3 image is now <u>shrunk back and down</u> to form a much smaller image in the centre of the page. Or rather like using a wide angle 28mm lens in your computer's Photo-Shop when joining images together to give a far distant panoramic landscape shot."

We now enter the area of <u>photomontages.</u> If you join a number of wide angle 28mmlens shots together you are going to produce a very acceptable image for 120 metre/400 feet high wind turbines being lost in the distance, or being shown as not truly representative.

In my opinion this further manipulation of the wind turbines images on the landscape to show how small the impact will be, and therefore giving the impression that people in the surrounding villages should not worry, is unrealistic and deliberately misrepresentative.

Here Nigel holds up various visualisations to support his case.

"Finally, Trans Energy's visualization team have made great emphasis in their Environmental Impact document, about having used Adobe Photo-Shop and other post-production graphic devices etc., to join and enhance these images together. This should not have been done or used, if you really want to attempt to give the public and Suffolk Council a realistic representation of how big or how small these wind turbines are really going to be.

To summarise: 'In other words these images have been <u>manipulated to show how little impact</u> these 120metre/400 feet wind turbines would have.'

To give four quick visual examples of the imagined heights of these turbines on the landscape surrounding our villages and Lower Victoria Farm, **<u>in your mind imagine superimposing</u>** any of the following on the landscape using a 50mm lens to give accurate representation.

**Here again Nigel holds up and shows individual pictures in the Council chamber.
<u>Imagine!</u>**

Big Ben in London at 311 feet.
The London Eye at 443 feet
The proposed wind turbines at 120metres/400 feet.
Norwich Cathedral standing at 315 feet

" *<u>Standing at 315 feet</u>* , Norwich Cathedral's spire is the second tallest in England, and dominates the skyline. Only the Spire of Salisbury Cathedral is higher at 404 feet, the same height as the proposed industrial wind turbines at Lower Victoria Farm. The proposed size of the five wind turbines at 400 feet/120metres would have a huge **<u>Visual Impact</u>** on this Suffolk skyline and would be seen for miles around dwarfing any residences, historical landmarks and churches into insignificance, and utterly changing the **<u>Character</u>** of this historic landscape.

Nigel now gives a long pause, hoping for dramatic effect and maximum impact.

" Like everybody else, I want the planet to survive, I have three grandsons. We are entering dark times regarding the production and consumption of energy. However, to build wind farms willy-nilly, tearing up tranquil rustic environments in the process, and erecting giants industrial wind turbines, is unlikely to solve our energy problems, or realistically meet many of the renewable energy targets.

As is often quoted in the press and TV, land wind farm production is only around 22% on average , of their possible <u>projected</u> generating capacity. So erecting five huge wind turbines opposite my house at Beshall is not going to solve these energy requirements. Nor would erecting a further proposed 166 land wind turbines in inappropriate residential areas in Suffolk, help solve national renewable energy targets.

And then there is of course the problem of the wind <u>not</u> blowing. Also economies of scale go straight out the window, with such a low number of wind turbines as proposed in this current planning application of five turbines only. Large land wind farms have been sited in clusters of ten or more on the barren hills south of San Francisco, in the windy hills of the Pas de Calais, Northern France, or along the sea wall in Holland or in the UK on our own windsweep hillsides and or on brown fill-fill industrial sites. The most successful in terms of hitting renewable energy targets are the wind turbines offshore with over a minimum of 25 turbines units, sited off the coast, even if the wind does not blow all the time!

According to Local Planning Policy Statement No. 5 'Planning For The Historic Environment' Issued by the Government under Policy HE 7 it states:

'Local planning authorities should take into account the desirability of new development making a positive contribution to the character and local distinctiveness of the historic environment. The consideration of design should include scale, height, massing, alignment materials and use.'

Nigel pauses, takes a breath and looks around at all the people in attendance, looks back to the lady Tribunal Inspector and continues.

"Suffolk Council have unanimously refused this revised planning application from Trans Energy Limited for these five huge industrial wind turbines at Lower Victoria Farm, on grounds of being totally inappropriate environmentally, if they were to be sited there. The majority of the village residents have overwhelmingly asked for refusal. There are three volumes of refusal letters.

I would therefore ask the Inspector conducting this Appeal by Trans Energby Limited, to also refuse the Appeal on similar grounds of visual impact and the effects on the local environment.

Thank you for your time."

Having delivered this statement Nigel walked back through the audience, attending the tribunal Appeal hearing. As he walked past people he knew he whispered some questions.

'Any good, did it all make sense?'

'Could you understand my visualisations statements alright?'

'Sorry was it a little too technical?'

People just nodded and smiled briefly, or just politely offered 'not bad'
as Nigel walked past back to his seat, thinking that most people there probably did not know what he was talking about.

Nigel then took his seat in the middle of the Council Chamber room with the Inspector immediately opposite, and with objectors to his right and the staff from Trans Energy on his left.

On the final day of the Appeal, Nigel discovered that if the appeal was granted certain Conditions would have to attached to this planning permission. From the way that these Conditions started to be discussed by both sides and the Inspector, it sounded to Nigel as if all was lost, and the appeal had been granted.

The public were allowed to ask questions about these planning Conditions during the hearing, after both sides had said their piece.

Nigel fretted about the development site, and was very worried that there might be an explosion during the excavation period due to the fact that there was still unexploded ordinance left in the fields opposite Beshall, from the Second World War by the American Air Force bomber squadrons who had been based near there, just down the road.

The energy company had one of the expert witnesses say that it was quite safe now, and all excavation works for the concrete bases of these huge turbines would be handled by expert engineers. All these explanations and justifications were all nicely wrapped up in Trans Energy's ten volume Environmental Impact documents.

Nigel raised his hand to speak.

'I am not an army man, but common sense would dictate that you would not disturb this area with unexploded ordinance left in the very site where these proposed wind turbines are going to be built, wouldn't it?'
enquired Nigel.

'Any comment or questions regarding this question from the public?'
the Inspector asked of the two opposing barristers and their legal teams sitting on the front rows.
'No madam,' the barristers replied in unison.

There were further questions about these Conditions with only vague or non-committal answers given. Then there was a lunch break. Nigel went for a swim and had a quick sandwich. On his return the Inspector was meticulously going through the remaining final Conditions to be meet should the Appeal succeed and planning permission was granted for the wind turbines.

Nigel thought he would ask one last question. It was to do with insurance indemnity and risk insurance. In the past all of Nigel's film productions had to carry expensive indemnity insurance covering everything under the sun, from health and safety to non-appearance of the actors.

'Before lunch I asked a question about unexploded ordinance on this proposed wind turbine site. I forgot to add that the main Transco Gas pipes run right through the middle of this site. If there was an explosion from this unexploded ordinance during excavation, and the main gas pipeline blew there would be no Lower Victoria Farm, no Beshall, not many of the surrounding villages left, and no Trans Energy site workers alive. Total wipeout! Is there any level of indemnity insurance included in these final conditions to cover such a contingency?'

'Any comments regarding this last question?' The Inspector asked both sets of barristers and their legal teams.

'No Madam,' said the Appeal barrister sheepishly.

'Not at this stage, Madam,' mumbled the Defence barrister.

The Inspector then moved on to the final Condition. It was now Friday afternoon, Nigel had had ten days of this. He wondered whether he was in the mad house, certainly nobody seemed to care about his last question. It was all water under the bridge and he was only a member of the public and therefore seeming to be less eligible in this planning scheme of things.

Time passed. To date there has been no final decision given by the Inspector on this Appeal, due to a huge back log of similar Appeals in the system. Plus the Government is changing its view on renewable energy. This has become political ammunition for the Government. Recently the Minister of the Environment has taken over making decisions over these final Appeals.

As a result property prices are not looking too healthy in the area where Nigel lived. In spite of this, a number of people in the surrounding villages have put their houses up for sale.

Nigel and his wife Pauline were among those people. After a quick reduced sale, they are now moving back to a much smaller house, a semi-detached one in the suburbs of North London.

Apparently, they are looking for peace and quiet again.

VIOLENCE

Six months before I moved out of London to the country to play out an urbanite's rustic dream, I was living in North West London, in a posh suburb called Belsize Park. I was the poor relative living in a tiny mews house off Haverstock Hill.

I asked a television director mate, when he came round with a bottle of wine, what he thought of this little mews house which had no garden or windows at the back,

'Cave dwelling mate,' was his reply.

'Thanks, another glass ?' I said, thinking 'what an arsehole'.

Well in order to get out from this cave, I used to go walking in one of London's loveliest parks, and then quite often to a pub called the Queen's in Primrose Hill. I was there with my wife Liz, and an old mate, John, from the hotel business discussing how things were going for him. It was Sunday afternoon on a nice warm spring day. I was thinking of having another pint, but I was doing the cooking, a roast chicken, as it happens.

'Well, I better nip back to turn the chicken and roast spuds, don't want anything burnt. You two have another drink, I'll see you up the road shortly,' I said.

I walked away from the pub, feeling relaxed and warm. Those good to be alive feelings that spring brings on. I turned a corner on a quiet residential street with a block of flats overlooking some rather expensive detached houses, with motor cars to match. Opposite the entrance of the flats I noticed three teenagers, fifteen or sixteen plus, trying to break into a car. I tend to react fairly promptly to things like this, which could be my downfall.

'What are you doing ?' I asked one of the kids.

'Fuck off you old git, mind your own business.'

'It is my business, I live round here, these are my neighbours and their cars.'

'Well aren't you a lucky bastard then.'

'It's not that, I just don't think you ought to break into people's cars.'

'You haven't got a clue, you have no idea about our lives, have you?'

'Don't suppose I have, but two wrongs don't make a right do they?' I said retreating up the street, and passing a large builder's skip in the street.

Suddenly I feel a dull thump in the middle of my back. They have picked up bits of old plaster out of the skip and are hurling them at me. I duck. Having started life off at a boarding a school in Hertfordshire, when I was just seven years old, I had learnt to fend for myself.

One of my accomplishments at this school was being good at sod fights, i.e., you rip up a great chunk of grass and earth and hurl it at the opposition. So, same thing, but no teachers to interfere or to stop any fights. I give return fire, hurling one bit of plaster after another. Starts to get a bit steamed up, but these kids are somewhat taken aback by my defence, almost turning into an attack. I gradually retreat up the street to the sound of

'Old tosser, fucking cunt.'

'You know I could get the police,' I yelled back.

'What good would that do, we'd be long gone.'

'There'd get you in the end.'

'Wanna bet, we'd get you lot first.'

'Yeah, yeah....' I mumbled as I turn the corner of the road that leads down to the little mews house where I live, thinking about whether I should I have done what I just did, and probably burning the chicken as a result.

I realised that I was trembling and had managed to frighten myself. What is one supposed to do, run away, hide under a bush, or just turn the other way and let them get away with suburban stealing.

Maybe get it in perspective, all property is theft and that.

One time in the late 1970's, I had worked for a couple of years in Nairobi in Kenya. If the Africans caught a robber in broad daylight, like these kids, there was not a lot of mercy or social understanding shown.
The robber often received a beating before the police arrived, and then they gave him another one. The police used to shoot car thieves on sight.
But on the other hand the thieves then started arming themselves and shooting back. Not so good.

'Bollox to that, do what you have got to do,' I said to myself.

I look around for something to defend myself with or even give somebody a good whack with. London suburban streets are full of builders' rubble and waste. I pick up a useful ex-floorboard, and
hung around the corner, waiting for the first teenager to appear.

Fortunately they did not appear. I have no idea what I would have done, probably whacked one of them, the other two would have jumped me, knifed me and I would have ended up one sad old git, stuck like a pig on a Sunday afternoon in the suburbs, with my wife and friend thinking
I was looking after Sunday lunch.

Alternatively, these kids could have gone to the police and said that I had attacked them in some crazy moment, and I would not have had a leg to stand on, there being no witnesses, and they being minors. I would have ended up in the slammer, charged with causing grievous bodily harm or common assault.

I put the floor board down and walked home. Opened the front door which was straight off the street, thinking about trite things like an Englishman's home is his castle, but this little place would take some defending against the marauding masses.

Checked the chicken and poured myself a glass of wine, wondering about chance, fate and making costly mistakes in life.

Liz and John came back shortly afterwards.

'Fabulous day, chicken smells good,' John said.

'I nearly got killed coming back.'

'What are you talking about now,' Liz asked.

'You know those little sods, who keep hanging around and breaking into people's cars?'

'Yes..'

'Well, I confronted them on the way home as they were breaking into a car round the corner. Ending up having a sod fight, chucking lumps of old plaster out of a builder's skip at each other. I felt like killing them. Got myself a bit of old floorboard, was ready to do battle, but they disappeared.'

'You're mad, fifty three years old and you still think you can have a go,' Liz said sharply.

'You did play rugby in the first fifteen in your school didn't you?' John asked, trying to wind me up even further.

'Ha, ha.'

'Why didn't you just call the police like any normal sane person?'

'What's sanity got to do with it? The first sign of a police car or its siren and they're off. What is one supposed to do in these lawless times?'

'Behave like a responsible adult, rather than a lawless hooligan.'

'Quite a good description of you really,' John said laughing loudly.

'I know my place, I'll go and make the gravy for this lovely lunch of ours,' I said, stomping off into the kitchen.

Six months later we were gone from the city. Bought an old beamed sixteenth century cottage in Suffolk, with a lovely half acre garden, got some real live chickens and started to grow our own vegetables. We had down sized even more in the city by just getting a small studio flat in a block of flats, which we rented most of the time. What we now called 'right-sizing.'

Recently I was back in north west London checking out a leaking pipe in this flat with the plumber. Afterwards, at around three in the afternoon, I thought I'd go down to the Queen's, the old pub opposite Primrose Hill, round the corner from where we lived. A trip down memory lane.

As I was driving, I had an expesso, so I was possibly more alert, whilst I listened to a couple of the locals rabbiting on about betting and horse racing. Their conversation went something like this.

'You know the betting shop on Haverstock Hill?'

'Yeah? which one?'

'The one near the Steeles' pub.'

'Yeah, I know that one, Corals isn't it?'

'That's it. Well I heard they got turned over today. Took some five hundred quid.'

'It's the times we live in. The recession and cut-backs that is causing it all. The police ought to stop it.'

'They try to. But that's not the only one that's been turned over. They did another couple of betting shops too. It's all the cash they carry, taken from the punters who bet and lose, like us.'

'What are we supposed to do, stop betting?'

I had just about had enough of this conversation, was just folding up my newspaper, when three older teenagers boys walked in through the other pub door. I recognized them as the three kids from that Sunday warm afternoon a few years ago. They were much more grown up now and big lads. I did not try to make eye contact at all, just quietly observed them. But I remembered them from that crazy moment on that warm Sunday.

The biggest of them steps up to the bar, turning to the other two kids.

'What are you having, I am buying. Bit of a result that,' he said producing a big wodge of rolled up twenty pound notes.

'Yeah, wasn't it? Pint of the Old Speckled Hen for me.'

'And for me too, got a bit of a thirst on, after that,' said the third teenager, smiling all over his face.

'We will just have to keep up the good work then, won't we boys?'
said the biggest one, handing out the beers.

Democracy

In March 2008, I was taking a car ride outside Melbourne on the road to Ballarat in the State of Victoria. I was accompanied by a well known lady Australian playwright, and her husband. I was doing some research for a First World War film about an Australian soldier. The soldier had been born in Ballarat. He had been an artist before the War. He was partially blinded in the War, the film was to be about his subsequent life after the First World War in Melbourne, and how he survived it all.

I was sitting in the back of a Volvo Estate car, with the playwright's husband who was an Australian history academic, quizzing him about Ballarat's history. He explained and elaborated on the Australian Gold Rush, which had been centred around Ballarat, and it seemed to have a connection to the early beginnings of real democracy in Australia. I thought this whole subject area would make an interesting story, and should be adapted into a film or possibly a novel. To date, the film has not been made nor has the novel been written. Here is the outline story:

'THE BALLARAT BOYS'

Caption: San Francisco, USA 1851.

The film opens on California's golden corn fields, set against rocky outcrops, outside San Francisco. However, there seems to be a cold atmosphere in this land, giving off a feeling that it has been spattered with the blood of its laborers. Injustice is in the air. Snap shots of extreme poverty, Mexican and Chinese workers, displaced native Indians and White posses intermingle, as the boundaries of 'Americanism' and 'whiteness' are being policed. Some vigilantes are hanging two Mexicans outside a gold mining camp, where there appears to be enforced Indian labor, whilst some Anglo-Saxon men sit around listening to one of them reading from a pamphlet entitled ' Sons of Manifest Destiny'.

Mix through to a small but rapidly growing downtown San Francisco. A group of politicians and businessmen are meeting in a prominent building, talking about law and the state, foreigners in California and the need for control and reform. This is the 1851 Vigilance Committee of San Francisco. In a bar opposite, two rugged looking young men are having a beer and talking earnestly. Sam Dixon is an Australian from Ballarat, and Johnnie Hague is a settler from back East.

They have met up in the Gold Rush of 1849. They discuss their luck to date, and what now seems to be happening in San Francisco.

Sam mentions the arbitrary lynching of an Australian thief called John Jenkins, and then Johnnie talks about the 'Sidney Ducks' mainly Irish Australians blamed for arson and crime in San Francisco, who followed Jenkins to the noose. They talk about the countryside where they found gold in California. Sam says that much of it reminds him of the hills and gullies back home in Australia, in Victoria and New South Wales.

Inside the Vigilance Committee is being addressed by an irate member Robert Brannan who shouts out "To hell with your courts! We are the courts! And the hangman!" Another member, William Sherman, a San Francisco banker adds that "as we control the press, we can write our own history."

Sam and Johnnie ride towards the docks in downtown San Francisco, past some heroic bourgeois vigilantes who are buckling on their six-guns to restore order. What they see is a society over-run by criminal immigrants and corrupt politicians.

Sam and Johnnie have had enough. They have made some money from their gold diggings. They take ship to Australia and Sydney, still hoping to further their fortunes.

In a bar in Sydney, there is much talk of a Gold Rush in Bathurst at Summerhill Creek, in New South Wales, and of a mass exodus from Sydney to the gold fields. The Governor of New South Wales wakes up, calls for his breakfast, gets no reply. All his staff have disappeared in search of 'the colour' as gold was called, at the Rush in Bathurst. Sam and Johnnie see a half empty Sydney and a harbour with abandoned ships. It is a gold fever. They take stock. When Sam takes a leak he overhears an old timer talking about more gold being found in Ballarat, in Victoria. There are so many rumours.

The two young men are seen riding across the outback in Victoria in the area outside Ballarat. Fade back picture, and roll on caption which is sung as it comes onto the screen:

> 'The night too quickly passes
> And we are growing old,
> So let us fill our glasses
> And toast the Days of Gold;
> When finds of wondrous treasure
> Set all the South ablaze,
> And you and I were faithful mates
> All through the Roaring Days.'
>
> (Henry Lawson)

Cut to close up shots of the two riders, galloping through low cover, a shallow stream, up and over a hill, disappearing out of sight.

Mix through to a long shot of a plain outside Ballarat, and in the distance the two riders heading for a large gold diggers' camp outside Ballarat town. They wear side arms. They are full of life and zest, and part of the great Gold Rush that is taking place in Victoria.

Mix on title: over a background of a very large diggers' encampment. It is the Eureka goldmine, outside Ballarat. Sam 'Digger' and Johnnie 'California' ride proudly through the camp, nodding to acquaintances, getting smiles from some of the few females in the camp, and a nod of approval from the men who are in charge:

'THE BALLARAT BOYS'

All around there is a sense of bustle and activity, a lot of happy faces, small groups of men moving off or coming back to the encampment, makeshift gold weighing stations, armed guards, authorities issuing mining licences, money passing hands, men looking at maps, pointing, recounting stories about gold discoveries, a feeling of a new and swelling population, good eating and drinking, a convulsion, that is driving this whole encampment of 1,000 plus diggers dangerously forward. It is the height of the 'Gold Fever'.

Sam 'Digger and Johnnie 'California' are two of the best 'diggers'.

Mix through to spinning newspaper headlines from those times. Headlines declare:

'Religion is neglected, education despised, the libraries are almost deserted.....

The new State of Victoria is full of adventurers from all round the world.....foreign Chinese invaders.....Americans with guns are a danger to our communities...monthly mining licence fees are too high.....'

Close in on headline '....Church men declare that the Gold Rush is a ruinous inundation, good settlers and citizens have been turned into wanderers, communities into mobs....'

Cut to Sam 'Digger' and Johnnie 'California' dismounting and tying up their horses, by their tent at Eureka. Like many others these two young men have had a wonderment, a rapturous obsession with voluptuous riches, with 'the colour' awaiting them in the Australian soil. They have dreamt of gold, they have found gold, they are surrounded by gold and all its trappings. They are young men of their time: 'Gold had been all in all to them.'

But this is no rich man's paradise. These 'Fossickers', these gold hunters, around Ballarat in late 1851, are subject to changes in their fortunes too. There is talk about bushrangers and an invasion of Chinese immigrants. In the background a Chinese family tends a very neat vegetable garden, whilst some of their produce is being sold to miners.

Sam and Johnnie sit around eating, and talking about the changing times around Ballarat. They say the gold may be running out. They decide to trek to one of the more remote 'diggers' outposts.

Next morning Harriett Holden, a young women who is living out on the gold fields with some of her family, approaches Sam and Johnnie, and asks about going along with them, with her friend from England, Ellen Dacy. Ellen comes over to them.

They are both dressed as men and have short cropped hair. They say they just want to stake their own claim and to pan and dig for gold. They have heard that Sam and Johnnie are experienced miners and know the terrain. Johnnie says that he does not think that diggings are for women. Sam says that they seem to be able to look after themselves, and that they are not really like California Widows, left defenceless. But it is best, if Johnnie and he search out this new goldfield and that Harriett and Ellen stay on this camp outside Ballarat. Perhaps next time. They will let them know. The women turn away, and whisper that all gold miners are liars.

Sam and Johnnie set out, arriving two days later feeling tired and thirsty. It looks a rough place, with trees torn down and filthy streams. Everything sacrificed for gold. They meet some of the other diggers, swap stories and get a licence, go to work & stake a claim. It is a rough old mining site, tough working, having to mine and dig down deep for any gold.

Time passing. They strike on some gold dust and smaller pieces, and next day on a big nugget of gold. They cannot believe their luck. After final diggings, they head off to Ballarat, to get their gold weighed and sold. They invite Harriett and Ellen over to a small miners' bar. They dance, drink grog, dream and plan. But behind their fun there is jealousy and whispered rumours from some other miners. The camp is a strange mix of adventurers, wanderers, immigrants, Chinese gardeners and possible bushrangers.

There does not seem to be enough police to control this ever growing camp. Johnnie and Sam are glad to leave. They tell Harriett and Ellen that they are going to Melbourne to buy some land to build on, but they will be back to take them to their gold field. Meanwhile, they should take out mining licences as soon as possible before the word of 'the homeward bounder' or large claim is found out.

Just outside Ballarat they are ambushed by bushrangers, beaten up and robbed of everything. They manage to keep two small nuggets of gold. They are now nearly destitute. They report the crime to the police who say they are fed up with all these crazy diggers claiming that they have been robbed all the time. The police say there are not enough police, to deal with all the crimes being committed by all these ex-convicts from Van Dieman's Land, and thousands of Chinese immigrants, foreigners and the likes of all these gold crazy diggers and now 'forty-niners' from California. The police captain tells them to get some proper work, and not to bother them again.

Sam and Johnnie do not know what to do. They try to set up again, but find it hard to start, it seems the word is, that the Ballarat gold is running out. Sam and Johnnie meet up with Harriett and Ellen who tell them about the harsh new mining licences coming in the new State of Victoria. Johnnie 'California' tells Sam about American history and 'no taxation without representation'. Sam quizzes him. Then they get their two last little nuggets of gold weighed in Ballarat. They get swindled at the weigh-in. The police are called. Sam and Johnnie are moved on. Harriett and Ellen look on helplessly.

Sam and Johnnie start to live rough in Ballarat. They meet up with some political groups who talk about political representation in the new State. To Sam and Johnnie it all seems a little cloak and daggerish. They hitch a ride to Melbourne.

On the way out of Ballarat, they stop at a small coaching station, where there are many soldiers and police, milling around. There is rather an intimidating atmosphere. Some of the mounted police make comments about immigrant trash and opportunist gold diggers. Sam and Johnnie are glad to leave, and to be going to Melbourne. The coach disappears over the horizon, leaving Ballarat in the setting sun.

Cut to old Melbourne laid out like a slick grid, appearing to be rich and prosperous in the centre. Johnnie and Sam are seen in a poorer tented quarter. Many immigrants are seen coming up from the port, walking past with hope written all over their faces. Sam andJohnnie stagger past them, into another grog-shop, singing. They have had a few.

They are at their wits end, wondering what they are going to do for money. Johnnie mentions about joining up to one of the new gold escorts, that are protecting the diggers' gold from robbers. They are hoping that they might catch the guys who robbed them outside Ballarat.

They ask to enlist in 'Dight's Light Cavalry', set up by a group of Melbourne business men who seem to be concerned that all these robberies are precipitating a financial crisis. Some of the business men say that private armies are a thing of the past and are unconstitutional. Dight and his cronies see an opportunity to calm the situation. They need young men like Johnnie and Sam. CR Dight is the boss. He is very selective in whom he chooses. There is some discussion as to whether Sam and Johnnie should be taken on. They are tested on their riding abilities and swordsmanship. Dight's decision is final.

A guard of twelve is chosen, with eight gentlemen, one sergeant who has been in the mounted police, and Sam and Johnnie as they know the gold field routes, and because they want to see justice done after their robbery. The last member of the Cavalry is a cook. Later, some of the officers in this cavalry are seen walking through the streets of fashionable Melbourne 'with jingling spurs, swaggering sabers and jaunty carriages'. The sergeant is put in charge of Sam and Johnnie. They do not like him, and he does not like them, and tells them so.
He calls them digger scum. This sergeant had spotted them at the small station outside Ballarat.

Dight's Light Cavalry rides out towards Ballarat, to protect a valuable consignment of gold nuggets coming in for weighing, to Ballarat. The sergeant niggles Johnnie and Sam as they ride along. They get to Ballarat. Amidst a tense atmosphere the gold is unloaded and weighed.

Later there is a skirmish with the sergeant and some diggers, near where the gold has been weighed. Guns are drawn, and in so-called self defence, the sergeant shoots two diggers dead. The sergeant then turns on Sam and Johnnie, and accuses them of attempting to rob this gold consignment, to get their own back on the owners of this gold, whom the sergeant falsely says, robbed Sam and Johnnie of their gold. They deny this vehemently, and after a struggle, they are over-powered, and are put into a holding cell.

Ellen and Harriett ride into Ballarat and rush to see them.

Dight is called back from a hotel where he has been drumming up more patrol work and enjoying his new found swanky success. It is late and getting dark, Harriett and Ellen leave. Sam and Johnnie decide that the odds are against them, break out through the roof of the holding cell, take their two Dight's horses and leg it back to Melbourne. As they race towards Melbourne, they roar with laughter, at least they are free and still alive.....

Cut to a 'Wanted' sign being nailed to a Eucalyptus tree, in Ballarat. Cut to the words that state 'one digger from Melbourne and one 'forty-niner' from California, are wanted for gold robbery and causing the death of two diggers'.

Cut to the faces of Sam 'Digger' and Johnnie 'California', on the poster. A crowd gathers round at dusk, many of them know and like these two young men, some of them start mumbling about police brutality. Harriett and Ellen are there. Harriett says that this sergeant was a well known bully, when he was in the Mounted Police before joining 'Dight's Light Calvalry'.

An old digger shouts out that they are only gold prospectors like us, 'Ballarat Boys' all and one. Ellen says 'And Ballarat Girls'. People laugh and press forward.

A good roaring cheer ensues, and they start singing:

'We be the aristocracy now....and aristocracy now we be...'

Many of the crowd head towards a grog shop. In the shadows they are watched by three men who try to appear to be part of the crowd. They are political agitators, a Prussian republican, Frederick Vern, a fiery Italian Redshirt, Raffaelo Carboni, and a blunt Scottish Chartist, Tom Kennedy. From a distance, a young Irish engineer watches the whole thing. His name is Peter Lalor who is leader of the newly formed Reform League.

Caption: One Year later, 1852, Melbourne, Victoria.

Cut to a faded newspaper headline: '……Gold diggings disorganize society…'

Sub-Heading: '…….gold diggings induce a moral blight, and gold diggings divert activity from saner enterprise…..'

In the corner of the faded newspaper is a small 'Wanted Sign' for Sam 'Digger' and Johnnie 'California'.

Cut to Sam 'Digger' and Johnnie 'California' sitting in a bar in a poorer quarter of the newly affluent Melbourne, with Harriett and Ellen. It is early evening. Sam and Johnnie have altered their appearance, both have grown beards, wear hats and sit a little apart. They keep a furtive eye on the door, more nervous than they were. They are still on the run. The girls know this.

They work down at the docks where nobody asks too many questions. Johnnie 'California' tries to not speak with an American accent any more. When the two men say goodbye to the women, they talk about meeting later that evening. They say they have got some important work to do at the docks. Laughter and sunshine return to their faces, as Sam and Johnnie wave goodbye to them.

Sam 'Digger' and Johnnie 'California' enter a large basement hall near the docks. The place is filled with men smoking; somebody is just finishing speaking on the wooden platform, about the need for political representation in the State of Victoria. Good round of applause. Another speaker gets up and talks about the need to get away from England and Queen Victoria and the British Government's heavy-handed policy about still sending convicts to Australia. Then a digger gets up and demands justice and fairness, and the vote for the gold mining communities...it is they who are building the new Melbourne.

Sam and Johnnie move round the room, they have been here before. They shake hands with Peter Lalor and some of his people from the Reform League. They talk privately.

In the background, Raffaelo Carboni, the Italian Redshirt takes the floor and talks about revolution and changing the state. After him, Tom Kennedy, the Scottish Chartist steps up. Peter Lalor, Sam and Johnnie turn to listen. Tom Kennedy declares:

> '...Moral persuasion's all a humbug,
> Nothing convinces like a lick in 'the lug.......'.

At this, Sam 'Digger' and Johnnie 'California' look at each, say they have got to go to work, and leave quickly. Tom Kennedy continues in the background. As they are leaving the hall, and walking round the corner, some mounted police arrive, heading towards the hall. Sam and Johnnie run for it. Later we see them talking earnestly through a smoky window of a bar with Harriett and Ellen. Outside, a policeman is watching them.

Next evening Sam and Johnnie are in the same bar with the girls. The men are more relaxed, more like their old selves, they flirt seriously with Harriett and Ellen, they laugh and declare their love and talk about marriage, when they will be rich again.....the girls pick up on this....to divert attention and suspicion, the men talk about Sydney and New South Wales, and maybe that is the place to be, and where they all should be heading for.

The women excuse themselves, go to powder room and talk agitatedly about their men. Ellen says that they are the 'Ballarat Boys', and that they are still 'wanted'. Harriett agrees, says marriage is out of the question. At the same time Sam 'Digger' and Johnnie 'California' are arguing about letting it slip, that they were rich once, before they were robbed. They should not have reminded the women again.

Sam says maybe it is time to split, go their own ways, Johnnie says he thinks he may go back to California. He says he could not have any worse luck than here. They decide to meet up in Sydney, but to travel there separately, and work it out from there.
They think there are too many police around looking for political agitators, and their chances of getting picked up, are increasing by the moment.

When Harriett and Ellen come back into the bar, they look around for them, but they have fled. In an alleyway, Sam and Johnnie say goodbye. They arrange to meet in Sydney, down at the docks. They have both decided to go to San Francisco, where they feel they can live as free men again.

Outside the same policeman, who spotted them the night before, is bringing round some reinforcements, hoping to catch Sam 'Digger' and Johnnie 'California'. He shows a 'Wanted' poster to the other policemen and points to the bar. As Johnnie 'California' is walking away on the other side of the road, he is spotted by the police. He runs for it, ducks up an alleyway, doubles back, sprints like fury, and dives into a door way. A hand grabs him, and pulls him in. It is Sam 'Digger'.

The police burst into the bar and after an argument drag off Harriett and Ellen as accomplices.

Sam and Johnnie get away on horseback, and head towards Sydney. They talk about what has happened to them, and what seems to be happening to many of the poorer folk in Victoria. They talk about the 'gold fever' that once possessed them. They look at each other, laugh and move from a canter to a gallop, as the light fades. Their journey is not easy. It is long, hot and arduous. Johnnie and Sam keep a low profile on the journey. They pass many wanderers, poor people and bushrangers. They show their side arms.

Meanwhile Harriett and Ellen are brought before a magistrate, who dismisses their case because of lack of evidence and the fact that they are women. The magistrate tells them that they ought to be at home with a family, not running around with lawless gold miners. Perturbed and upset, they ride back to camp at Ballarat, pack up and ride out to the place where Sam and Johnnie said they had found their gold. They have got a new mining licence, and Sam's maps.

Cut to old Sydney port. Sam 'Digger' and Johnnie 'California' are looking round for a ship that might be going back to America. They wait around for a couple of days. They spot a freighter ship from San Francisco. They get some temporary dockers' work, and manage to get to unload a freighter ship, the S.S.Unity, from San Francisco.

They decide to stowaway on the S.S.Unity, working out a plan to get on board the ship in the early evening, when there are less guards on board. Before they do this they have one final meal in Australia. In the bar, Sam notices a headline about agitators being jailed in Ballarat, for causing trouble and political upheaval.

It seems that Peter Lalor and Tom Kennedy were among the people arrested. Sam and Johnnie talk about how they should have possibly stayed in Ballarat, and faced the music after they had been arrested. Johnnie says maybe they would have got off, been given a pardon. Sam disagrees, given the lack of voting power, the heavy handed government, and police in Victoria. They have a few drinks, and head down towards the docks and the S.S.Unity, which is getting ready to set sail for San Francisco.

Cut to the ship at sea in the Pacific, which is blowing up a little. The captain asks one of the crew to check the life boats. The crewman reports back to the captain and says that one of the life boats has been tampered with. The captain and three crewmen approach this life boat.

A brief scuffle ensues. Sam 'Digger' and Johnnie 'California' are back in a holding cell again. This time it is serious.

The captain is used to stowaways and exploiting them for their passage. But the captain also twigs that they might be wanted men. He cross-examines them separately, and his suspicions grow. He thinks there might be a price on their heads. Sam 'Digger' now calls himself Phillip Carter, and Johnnie 'California' calls himself Robert Cook. They had decided on this before they left Sydney. The captain decides to put them into irons, till he is satisfied about whom they actually are. It looks as if all is lost.

After a rough journey land is spotted. Old San Francisco comes into view. It is a fabulous looking city. Sam 'Digger' and Johnnie 'California' rot down below. They talk about jumping off the ship. Johnnie says that is sure death, either the cold currents will drown you or the sharks will get you.....he knows this part of the world.

The S.S. Unity docks in San Francisco. Two crewmen come to collect Sam and Johnnie. They are unshackled and a fight takes place. Sam and Johnnie are desperate. They take the two crewmen prisoner, and go to the captain's quarters where there is a stand-off. The captain says that they do not have a chance either here in America, nor back in Australia. He produces a Wanted poster from among a collection kept in his desk.

Sam 'Digger' and Johnnie 'California' inform the captain that they helped unload his ship in Sydney, and that they found out about his illegal shipments of arms being freighted from America to Australia, plus the racket the captain was also running, bringing in illegal immigrants.

The captain says prove it.....they hand him copies of a letter that they sent to the police authorities in Sydney. The letter does not mention the actual name of the ship. Sam and Johnnie say that if no word is heard from them in three months in Melbourne, then their 'wives' Harriett and Ellen will send the same letter again to the police authorities in Sydney, but this time mentioning the name of the ship and its captain. There is a stand off.

American Customs men board the ship, a crewman rushes to the captain to tell him what is happening. The US Customs come up to the captain's quarters and enter. Total change. The captain is quietly sitting down at his desk, with Sam 'Digger' going through some paperwork, whilst Johnnie 'California' looks out of a porthole.

Sam & Johnnie look innocently at each other. The US Customs guys know the captain well. They want their pay-off too.

<u>Caption:</u> San Francisco 1854.

San Francisco has changed and grown, but is still run by the Vigilance Committee.

Sam 'Digger' is working in a new bar and restaurant in downtown San Francisco. It is glitzy, glamorous atmosphere with plenty of girls, booz, good food, and dollars galore.

Intercut to Johnnie 'California' who is working at a new newspaper plant, type setting the latest edition of the San Francisco Chronicle.

Sam and Johnnie look like their old selves, no beards or disguises. They seem to be doing well. They meet up later in a corner of Sam's bar. They talk about Australia, and decide that the world has treated them badly, and that they were never fugitives, and that they want to get their names cleared, and to get a pardon. They have no idea how they are going to do this.

Nobody cares, and nobody certainly cares about them.

Mix through to Harriett and Ellen panning for gold by a riverside near Ballarat in Victoria, finding a small gold vein and tracing it to a small rocky outcrop, where they discover gold galore. Their success is blighted by not knowing about what is happening to Sam and Johnnie. They sit by the riverside, take out a crumpled photo of them, look at it and then at the gold in front of them.

Johnnie 'California' works on the San Francisco Chronicle, and is aware that the editor sometimes gets some syndicated world news. It is all a slow process. One day Johnnie is checking through the first edition of the newspaper, and spots an article about Australia. It is an article about an armed uprising in Eureka, near Ballarat in Victoria.

Various names are mentioned, some are supposed to be well known agitators, including Peter Lalor, Tom Kennedy, Raffaelo Carboni and Frederick Vern. The article states, that as the year 1854 was coming to an end, a thousand men assembled at Eureka, on the outskirts of Ballarat, and unfurled their flag, a white cross and stars on a blue field, to proclaim their oath:

'We swear by the Southern Cross to stand truly by each other, and fight to defend our rights and liberties....'

The article continues '.....troops from Melbourne overran the improvised stockade on the slopes of the Eureka goldmine and killed twenty-two of its defendants.....'

Johnnie is overwhelmed by what he reads next, and asks his boss if he could take a short break for fifteen minutes just to get some air. It is hot outside. Johnnie runs down the hill to show the article to Sam who is working away in his bar and restaurant.

Mix: Whilst Johnnie is reading this article and running to meet Sam, a continuous mix is run, showing the Eureka Stockade, troops approaching the Stockade, gold miners holding their Southern Cross flag up, singing, and being shot down in cold blood.

Johnnie 'California' rushes into the bar where Sam 'Digger' is pouring drinks for some dandily dressed Californian businessmen. He cannot contain himself. He rushes up to the bar.
Johnnie shows the newspaper article to Sam who looks rather confused. The American businessmen pick up on it, and say it sounds a bit like their own American Declaration of Independence is happening in Australia.

Sam says what use is it to them, they have left Australia, and it would not be any good if they tried to go back. Johnnie gets angry and says that is the trouble with Australians, they never listen and stomps off back to work. He slams the article down on a desk.

The second part of the newspaper article is revealed:

'.....The Eureka rebels have been vindicated. Juries in Melbourne have refused to convict the leaders put on trial for high treason, a Royal Commission condemned the corrupt goldfields administration. The miners grievances have been remedied, and their demands for political representation are going to be meet.......' The article concludes '....Peter Lalor, the rebel, is going to stand for parliament.....'

Sam 'Digger' and Johnnie 'California' meet up in Chinatown in San Francisco, and do not talk for a while. Sam smiles and says that if Peter Lalor gets into Parliament, maybe he could get them a pardon, after all they did not commit any crime to begin with, and then they were forced to go on the run.

Johnnie likes the idea, but wonders what he would do back in Australia. Sam thinks they ought to write to Peter Lalor and spill the beans that they are 'The Ballarat Boys' hiding out in California, even though they never committed any crime in the goldfields.

Cut to Peter Lalor, as a newly elected member of Parliament reading out Johnnie's and Sam's letter about how they did not commit any crime, but were forced to go on the run, by a corrupt, bullying ex-police sergeant who joined up with 'Dight's Light Cavalry.'

Lalor declares that it might be a good thing for the State of Victoria and Australian political stability, if diggers and even 'forty-niners' were given a pardon. He suggests that it would get the people on their side, get support for Parliament. Other members object violently, and it seems that Lalor's requests for pardons are very unlikely to happen.

Harriett and Ellen come out of a Bank, next to the Parliament building, and met up with Peter Lalor. They plead with him about trying to get a pardon for Sam and Johnnie. He is not optimistic. In Parliament again Peter Lalor speaks about the need for reform and the spread of democracy.

Cut to Sam 'Digger' and Johnnie 'California' arriving back in Ballarat. The crowds cheer, and yell a big welcome.

Sam and Johnnie stand at the back of a rostrum. Peter Lalor steps up to this make-shift rostrum. He welcomes 'The Ballarat Boys' back to a new and better land. In the crowd are Ellen and Harriett in tears. A rousing cheer and everybody starts to sing:

'The night too quickly passes
And we are growing old,
So let us fill our glasses
And toast the Days of Gold;
When finds of wondrous treasure
Set all the south ablaze,
And you and I were faithful mates
All through the Roaring days.'

Peter Lalor brings Sam and Johnnie forward, more cheers, and singing. Peter Lalor says that they have been pardoned and that they are free men. Later they ask him how he managed to get them a pardon.

Peter says that where there is a gold rush, there is going to be change, hopefully change for the better. Peter continues by saying that some people might say you two were a 'trade-off', for one of my moves towards a more democratic Australia.

Sam and Johnnie look at each other and say 'what's it matter we are free now' and they start laughing....

Ellen and Harriett, now dressed finely and sporting beautiful hair and makeup, rush forward from the crowd.

Sam andJohnnie do a double take, and then they embrace their girl. Harriett tells them about the gold they discovered, but says that 'it does not matter anymore'. The four of them look at each other, laugh and walk off.

Mix through to a fluttering Southern Cross Flag.

Over this, a rolling caption:

Many of the events in this film really happened:

The gold produced from the Australian Gold Rush meant that the Australian colonies were totally transformed economically and politically......

.....the gold produced from the Californian Gold Rush, meant that both America and the United Kingdom were able to secure their

currencies by going onto the Gold Standard, and thus underwriting their financial dominance in the world.

The Eureka Stockade and Rebellion was Australia's <u>only</u> armed uprising.

The Eureka Stockade is now viewed as the birthplace of Australia's political system and the establishment of democracy.

Sam 'Digger' Dixon settled in Ballarat and successfully established two hotels and a restaurant which are still there today. He married Ellen.

Johnnie 'California' Hague left for Sydney with his new wife Harriett, and was one of the founders of an Australian newspaper.

The End.

Melbourne/London

12th November 2008.

In Excelis Gloria

Early Sunday morning, light rain, south Norfolk, the small village of Bushton is awakening. Bernard, a fit looking man in his sixties cycles up to a single storey 13th century flint built church, in late February 2010. He carries a bible on the back of his bike. He quickly leans his bike up against the church yard gate, snatches up the bible, checks his watch and heads towards the medieval church door.

Bernard comes into the small nave of the church where there are a handful of other people in their sixties chatting.

'Sorry I am late' said Bernard to Mary, the female lay preacher.

Mary is a very laid back type of preacher, what some might call 'mother earth' with sermons to match. Bernard thinks she probably smoked pot in the 1960's.

'That's OK, we haven't started yet, here are your sheets for this Matins Service.'

'I prepared the three lessons to read, Luke, The Philippians and Genesis,' says Bernard, showing Mary a piece of paper, taken from his bible.

'Let's just read Luke and the Philippians for the lesson,' Mary said warmly smiling.

'Together in one reading ?' Bernard enquiried.

'Please...' Mary walked towards the altar of the church

A demure petite lady called, Julie, speeds past.

'You opened up the church and you seem to have done everything,
Julie ?' Bernard mumbled.

'Oh don't worry, I know where everything is. Liz alright ?' Julie enquired.

'Well actually, she seems to have a bit of a cold...this awful weather we have been having.'

Julie and Bernard move towards the left hand pews at the front of the church. Bernard sits by himself behind the others.

'Well quite a few more than last week,' declared Mary.

In the front pew are Harriett, a dark haired quiet woman and Julie. Behind them is Brian, a trendy retired teacher from North London, but with a strong Welsh accent, and next is Michael, a dark horse of an accountant who likes his beer, and sitting next to him his well-organized wife Jennifer. Behind them sits

Bernard moving up and down the pew, trying to avoid the cold shafts of air whistling down from the roof.

Suddenly the church door opens and in rushes Peter, an interior designer, who is still in his fifties and fashionably dressed including a berry which he keeps on. Peter sits down quickly next to Bernard who nods at him. Bernard is never quite sure whether Peter might be a little the other way, as he always seems to be rather excited when he sees Bernard who plays on this.

 'This should be fun,' snorted Peter to Bernard, as he moved up the pew to Bernard.

'Here at last Peter, now we can begin,' Mary said standing up. There is a very informal atmosphere, with a feeling of attempted or exaggerated togetherness.

Mary moves to the first pew where she has a portable CD music player and puts on a modern day hymn. Bernard makes out he is wincing in pain. Everyone starts to look through the order of the day which is made up of a prayer sheet for the beginnings of Lent, and a couple of extra sheets with two of the lessons printed out.

After the music stops Brian looks round at Peter who nods to him.

'Mary isn't there some important news we need to announce?' Peter asked.

'Well there is. That's true. The appointment of the new vicar to replace Janet who has now retired. His name is James Reeves and he starts in May,' Mary said.

'Not before May?' Brian asked.

'Well no,' Mary replied.

'What sort of fellow is he, where does he come from?' Peter enquired.

'From Enfield...' Mary replied.

'Err,...God,' Bernard whispered to Peter.

'At least he is a bloke,' said Peter smiling at Bernard.

'You mean breakdown the new female vanguard in the Church establishment and all that,' said Bernard.

'Perhaps we should Google this James Reeves to see who he is?' Peter cut in.

'That's not necessary, I have already looked him up on Facebook, there is plenty of information there,' Brian said to Peter.

'Wow you trendy thing, on Facebook, all the latest IT information to hand.' retorted Peter.

'That's me,' Brian said quietly.

'I think we will wait till May, and his arrival, now let's continue with the Service,' Mary said in rather an earthy and patronizing manner.

The initial prayers are read by Mary with this tiny congregation adding the 'Amens.'

This is the time for contemplation, for people to think about what has happened, what is happening and what will happen to them, in Norfolk, in England, in Europe and in the rest of the world. Just that one hour a week to get away from it all. Maybe pray a little, just think things over, review one's life a little, and possibly think of others less fortunate than one self.

That's the idea anyway.

Mary indicates to Bernard that it is now time for the lesson reading. Bernard leaps to his feet, Peter gets up to let him out of the pew whilst eyeing him, up and down. Bernard steps up to the lectern.

Bernard reads the first lesson which is Chapter 3 of the Philippians, which he thinks that he had not studied at his Catholic school, wondering about it, as he reads it , 'changing vile bodies and fashioning them into his glorious body...'

What does it all mean?

Bernard has worked in the film and television industry in London as a director and has also done some acting too, so this is little moment offers a chance to project his voice onto this ecclesiastical stage, to putting in some exaggerated pauses for dramatic effect, onto to an 'audience' that he knows well.

It comes to the last lesson reading, which is taken from Luke's Epistle Chapter 13, starting with:

'The same day there came certain of the Pharisees, saying unto him, get thee out, and depart hence: for Herod will kill thee...' Bernard thought back, remembering from when he was a kid, Herod always seemed to be an evil man.

Bernard continues: 'O Jerusalem, Jerusalem, which killest the prophets and stonest them that are sent unto thee; how often would I have gathered thy children together, as a hen doth gather her brood under her wings, and ye would not!'

Bernard finishes, thinking about Liz, his wife, and her rare breed collection of chickens down the road. It would have been good if Liz had come today, with this lesson partly being about chickens.

Peter gets out of the pew to let Bernard in.

'Super reading Bernard...' Peter whispered to Bernard.

'Oh really....find a lot of the bible rather confusing, also brutish and nasty...'

Mary plays another piped hymn out of her music box, closes this off with a prayer for the sick, and people in difficulties, mentioning the recent Chilean earthquake and the suffering people in Haiti. She puffs herself up for the sermon.

'Well, if you look at your sheets you will see the reading from Luke that Bernard has just read.'

Everyone shuffles through their paper handouts. Mary reads out the quote

'Jerusalem, Jerusalem which killest the prophets, and stonest them that are sent unto thee; how often would I have gathered thy children together, as a hen doth gather her brood under her wings, and ye would not!'

Mary steps forward to speak.

'Jesus is trying to protect us from the people who do not believe in him. He acts like a mother hen to protect us, his children. We all need help in this world, whether in old age, in life generally or when we are young children just starting out. It seems disease and disaster surround us, most of our lives. Think of the wars in Iraq, Afghanistan and the recent earthquakes in Haiti and now another one in Chile with a potential for a Tsunami to hit the coast of Japan at any minute now.'

'Some people are out there helping in their communities, whether it be aiding people in disaster zones or at home helping the aged and sick or working in social areas which benefit society. I know we have recently raised some funds for our church here, but where are the people who raised these funds, not in church I notice.'

'Jersualem, Jersualem . Shouldn't it be Bushton, Buston village rather ?' asked Mary.

The congregation look at each other.

'Some of us come to church, but how do we really protect our flock in Buston, our hens and chickens, this is really the big question.'

At this point Mary seems to fade away, as if she is some kind of actress who has forgotten her lines.

Harriett who is sitting quietly in the front pew, holds up a book.

'There is a picture reference here to Jesus and this passage from Luke about the chickens,' Harriett said to Mary.

'Oh, what book is that?' Mary asked.

'Stanley Spencer's paintings,' Julie replied.

'Stanley Spencer was off his rocker…!' declared Bernard to Peter.

'You are so educated Bernard,' Peter snapped back.

The Stanley Spencer book is passed around, and opened at a page where there is a portrait of Christ covering and protecting a hen and her brood. The book is passed back to Bernard and Peter.

'One of several portraits he did of Christ, pretty weird stuff,' stated Bernard.

'If you say so,' Peter said, passing the book back to Michael who shows the picture to his wife Jennifer.

The Service continues with The Our Father being read out loud, as a prayer. Mary finishes off the service with traditional Christian blessings being offered.

Bernard feels a sense of relief that it is over. Everyone rests in their pew before getting up to have a chat. Mary appears to be quite keen to get going. Bernard is thinking that there may be coffee which he wants to avoid, as he and Liz are supposed to be going to an early film showing , at a local arts venue at 12 noon.

Bernard makes his way to the back of the church to tidy up the service sheets and to check out the time and service details for next week, as one of his duties is to change these details on two magnetic boards just up the lane from the church. Whilst he is getting these magnetic strips together and checking them against a service rostra, Brian sidles up to him.

'Hi Bernard, funny old time this once a week thing,' he said quietly to Bernard, who thinks Brian is fishing for something, but does not know what.

'I don't know what I am doing here, I was brought up as a Catholic, went to a Benedictine school, and don't know whether I really believe in God. I read the epistles of St. Augustine and a lot of existentialism at university, gave up religion on philosophical grounds. Then I started to think along the lines of the possibility of a centralized state caring for society, but that didn't seem to work out from what we have seen in Russia and other communist countries, and so on.'

'Yes maybe, but I just don't get it, what was Mary going on about,' said Brian grinding on.

'Still it is time out, time to think things over for another week…..good thing about Catholics though, is that we go to church and then straight to the pub afterwards. I'd buy you a pint but it is a bit early, I don't think the pub is open yet,' Bernard said.

'Funny sermon. You know I come here for a bit of peace and quiet not to be provoked,' Brian retorted.

'Oh really. Sorry, excuse me, I'll just nip out, and pop these strips up on the boards for next week's service, back shortly,' Bernard said, looking past Brian and then darting out through the old medieval wooden church door.

'OK,' replied Brian.

Bernard rushes down the church path through the graveyard, eyeing up eighteenth and nineteenth gravestones with suspicion, and onto the road which is partially flooded from heavy rain. He changes the details on one of the outside boards, taking the new magnetic strips from his coat pocket and shoving the old strips into his other pocket.

He leaps across puddles but has to jump up on the other bank, as the road below is completely flooded. He is hanging onto to the notice board, changing the magnetic strips, trying not to drop anything into the water, when Mary zooms up in a newish 4 x 4 vehicle. Mary has an impish glint her eyes

'Thanks very much Bernard, good to see you in church,' Mary cried out lowering the window.

'Oh yes, see you again,' Bernard said politely.

'Nice jeep, why haven't I got one of those …? Because you're not a vicar…'
says Bernard talking to himself, whilst extricating himself from the flooded bank.

He nips up the path again and is met by the little congregation who seem to be now talking quite seriously in the porch with the main door shut behind

them, but with a half open iron grill door in front of them.
Brian is standing by the door. To Bernard it looks rather like some sort of animal cage at the zoo with a wooden door. The small congregation looks trapped.

'Who needs theatre or the playwright Alan Ayckbourn's 'Chorus of Disapproval' when we have this,' Bernard mouthed to himself, squeezing past Brian as he joins the rest of the small congregation in the porch area.

'Well, I've done that, stuck next week's times up, and Mary 's gone off in her new 4 x 4,' Bernard stated.

'That's it, who the hell does she think she is? I come here for a rest from the world, and to contemplate, not to hear Mary mouthing off about whether I have done enough for Buston village or the church,' clamoured Brian, looking round at the others.

'Really,' Bernard said quietly.

'Well you heard it Jerusalem, Jerusalem, Buston, Buston village, are we supposed to be the people who throw out the prophets, what was she going on about? I don't know whether I believe in the whole thing, I certainly don't want to feel criticized when I make the effort to come to church, that's all I am saying,' retorted Brian.

'I agree, I felt it was a bit rich, I mean we make quite an effort in this village you know. If it wasn't for us this would not happen,' said Peter tugging down his berry.

'Well we do need to help people less able than ourselves, and we all of us are so damn lucky that we live here, not in some hell hole with earthquakes or dictators, or up a high rise flat in a grimy city,' cut in Bernard.

'I did not see Mary's comments like that. We all need to contribute and do something. I think Mary was right in many ways,' Julie said rather purposely.

'I don't know. I don't do anything for this village, I don't protect any flocks or look after any old ladies. Except, I did that bit of part-time A Level Sociology teaching at Gunstan High School for a couple of years. Sort of giving back to the community. Mainly chop wood at home is what I do now and mow the lawn. Liz is good with all her village committee stuff like you Brian,' Bernard said sheepishly.

'Maybe, I just don't get it with Mary,' Brian said.

'It is food for thought though, it is not an easy situation trying to keep these small churches going,' Michael cut in.

'I find church is stimulating, and a place to meet, and think things over,' Jennifer said.

'Maybe we should write a letter to Mary complaining,' suggested Peter mischievously.

'Do you think so?' asked Brian

'What good is that going to do really?' demanded Julie.

'Do you know when I was teaching the Sociology of Religion to seventeen and eighteen year old girls?' Bernard begun.

'Enough of that,' cut in Brian.

'Well the Church of England was having one of its big Synods, with archbishops etc., from all over the world. All they seemed to go on about, was whether women could become Bishops and whether gays could become vicars or bishops. Who cares, we need to talk about Christian values. Certainly these kids were not impressed by these antics of this Synod, didn't care in my opinion. It was outside their framework. It was just Sociology in the end. Christian values did not come into to it,' lectured on Bernard.

'Sociology is a strange subject for a start,' Peter said smiling.

Harriett holds her Stanley Spencer book up.

'Strange how this artist painted this scene with Jesus and the chickens and we are talking about it now,'

Harriett said turning the pages to show the picture again.

'You bet,' Brian said, hanging onto the open iron grill door.

'Why don't you step outside Brian and lock us in the porch. We will still be here next week, continuing with this religious discussion?' Bernard chipped in.

'Ha, Ha, I meant what I said though, quite spoilt my Sunday,' said Brian.

'Mine hasn't started yet,' Peter said.

'Rock'n'roll,' quipped Bernard.

Bernard and Brian are the last to leave the church porch after the rest have moved off. Brian puts on his Wellington boots and starts to head off across a path through the graveyard.

'Different exit, Brian ?'

'Yep, it is quicker this way,' stated Brian.

'Yes I suppose it is,' agreed Bernard.

'Give me time to think things over, and all that,' said Brian.

'Time for a drink if you ask me, see yer,' Bernard said.

'Ciao Bernard,' said, Brian nodding and heading off across the path through the graveyard.

Bernard gets on his bike, starts to cycle round the back of the church on the village low road, in the same direction as Brian is heading for. Bernard sees Brian in the distance coming out of the graveyard. He carries on cycling.

'Well Brian does seem to have got a bee in his bonnet. He is meant to be a Christian. Wonder if he really knows the meaning of the word.....oh well,' said Bernard talking to himself, whilst he wobbles off on his bicycle, down along the small country lane.

Summer Exhibition

'Look Ye Also, Whilst Life Lasts.'

Nowadays older people seem to leave London, when they have had their fill, made their money, or are tired of the place possibly, and then head for a rural retreat or a quieter smaller town. It does not mean that one is tired of life, but that one is looking for something different, slower than inner city life.

Meanwhile the young do the opposite and pour into London. That's where the money is and where it is all happening. Add to this young immigrants and European migrant workers and you have a new face of London, all over again.

What seems to happen for many people over this geographical age dichotomy is that the older generation visit the younger generation in London for parties, other social events and very occasional overnights. Then the young people come out to see their parents in their rural retreats, coming to stay as if they have never really left home, wanting to feel cosy and safe, often getting waited on hand and foot.

This process seemed to have happened to Hugh Piers and his wife Petra, when they moved out of London to South Norfolk to a lovely old house with a few acres of land. Their nearest town was a well-known market town, had all the things people wanted in London, but often could not get. You could park easily, it had traditional shops such as butchers and green grocers, a compact super-market, some good pubs and an hotel, a couple of art galleries, theatre and cinema viewings in the local Corn Exchange and traditional Indian and Chinese restaurants. Hugh used to think what more could a man want. And no Tube trains either.

However, there was a pre-dominance of older people. A good friend of Hugh's, Paul who was still hanging on in London in a small terraced house in Battersea, had called this idyllic market town 'the old people's home'. Hugh did not think this was particularly funny. He sometimes called modern London 'one big parking meter'. His mate Paul in Battersea said that Hugh was missing out on all the culture and exhibitions in London, and all the fun. Paul was a serial bachelor.

In order to bridge this metropolitan gap, Hugh often used to go to London for the day on the railway and then get the Tube to South Kensington and go straight to Christie's auction rooms, view as much fine art as possible and then move up to the Royal Academy in Piccadilly, and then possibly visit the smaller galleries in the street opposite ending up at Sotheby's auction rooms, and again viewing the fine art auctions mainly.

Hugh was convinced that you could view more fine art in these conditions, than when struggling round a grand exhibition where one ended up having to queue up to view a picture. This was not for him. It seemed to make a mockery of art.

After these viewings Hugh might met some of his old London acquaintances in his London club, have a late lunch and a few drinks and then set off again on the train with lot of bleary eyed commuters who all seemed to fall asleep, as soon as they had got settled onto the train home.

As an alternative to this Hugh would often go on-line to these major auction houses and see what they were selling in London and New York. He often thought that some of the works classified as 'contemporary' were not that good or possibly somewhat pretentious. But that did not seem to matter, as they all seemed to command very high prices, with $50,000 being a very low marker on most works for sale in one New York auction of twentieth century paintings and sculpture.

But there was a certain method in Hugh's madness. His daughter Cathleen who lived in California with her family had turned out to be a brilliant portrait painter, possibly following some family artistic trait.

Hugh's mother, who had attended St. Martin's School of Art, was an accomplished artist, and had been a top dress designer in the 1930's. Hugh had studied film and television at a top art school in London, but had not really been into drawing and painting. Cathleen had studied fashion in London too, but Hugh thought that it was in her portrait painting where her strengths lay.

He thought that his daughter Cathleen just 'had it', that she could capture a portrait, an image particularly getting the unique look in people's eyes which great artists seem to have the ability to capture. Her portraits were like nothing else, and reminded Hugh of portraits done by Rembrandt, Gainsborough, Goya, Van Gogh and Picasso.

He had tried to get some of her works sold in San Francisco, and trolled around the various galleries off Union Square. But he did not seem to get anywhere, though he could see that one or two dealers were intrigued by some of her works. It was also about reputation Hugh realized.

So he went to see one of the valuers at Christie's in South Kensington, with a view to selling her work in England. Hugh did a small presentation of his daughter's works. The valuation expert was impressed but said that Cathleen was not quite ready for selling at this famous auction house. He suggested a couple of people to represent his daughter . He also mentioned the Summer Exhibition at the Royal Academy. The valuation expert implied that a good artist had to have had works shown at the Royal Academy to give their works credence or a kind of public provenance.

So Hugh made an investigation into the Summer Exhibition held at the Royal Academy every summer. According to their website there were some twelve thousand entrants, with twelve hundred being chosen, and a chance for one hundred new entrants to be chosen. The elected Royal Academicians were well represented too. One was allowed to enter two paintings, or photographs, prints, drawings, sculptures or architectural models at twenty five pounds per entry.

Hugh did all the relevant research on-line and then forwarded it to Cathleen in San Francisco. This was in November the deadline for entry was March ready for the grand opening in June. The summer Exhibition ran for three months till August with over two hundred thousand visitors attending , plus you could sell you work there with Royal Academy taking a commission.

Hugh went to Thanks Giving in San Francisco and tried to rev the whole thing up. They talked about what she might enter for the show and left it at that. After Christmas Hugh started emailing again to Cathleen saying that it was fairly urgent to get the forms filled in and send her two chosen portraits over.

It then materialized that there was some difficulties with overseas entrants. Hugh tried to reason that Cathleen could apply from his Norfolk address, but to no avail.

As a result Hugh thought that he would do a 'dry run' himself and enter a couple of his own portraits, done in pencil and colour washes, into to the Summer Exhibition. Also, it was made easy, as it was all terribly well organized by the Royal Academy.

Hugh was in the RA system and received his entrance packet with important paperwork, labels and supermarket type bar-codes identifying the works you had entered.

Hugh had done a small portrait in the style of a Paul Klee painting, of a surprised looking girl with squiffed up hair, entitled 'Ooh, La, La' in pencil and colour wash, which he painted the year before in the depths of winter when he thought he would try out some portrait painting too.

The other portrait that he entered was taken from a newspaper photograph of a Jewish girl who was rescued in 1938 from the Germans, who had just landed in England. She had plaits and looked very sad. It was another pencil and colour wash and was entitled 'Etcetera'. On the back of each portrait was a further label and then some more paperwork to be handed in when you entered your works at the Royal Academy.

Hugh travelled down to London, with his two portraits in a suitcase. He queued round the back of the Royal Academy, opposite Saville Row, and went down some steps through a covered eighteenth century Georgian entrance. Inside it was set up a bit like an old fashioned customs checking area, with several very pleasant and efficient young staff checking people's work in.

On the way out Hugh saw some other entrants carrying in some very large paintings, looking more like real artists should do. Hugh thought that they all looked a little miserable, and made some encouraging remarks to the even longer line of entrants queuing right into the street now . After a few drinks in his club telling some of the staff that he entered the Summer Exhibition at the Royal Academy, Hugh caught a taxi to the station, and got the train home.

A few months went by and then Hugh received a letter from the Royal Academy saying that his two works had not been chosen, that he needed to collect his paintings, and indicating when he could collect them.

A few weeks later, it just so happened that Hugh's ex-wife Giselle was having a sixtieth birthday party at her daughter's flat in West London, so Hugh decided it would make sense to collect his paintings from the Royal Academy, see the Summer Exhibition and then go on to the party. He and his wife Petra were then going to stay the night with friends.

So Hugh and his wife, Petra spent the afternoon at the Summer Exhibition, were suitably impressed by many of the paintings, photographs, prints, architectural models and some of the sculpture works. They left with the brochure outlining the main exhibitions in the various salons and a list of the elected Royal Academicians who were allowed to exhibit up to five works of art each .

Later that day, Hugh, Petra and George, an old friend from New York, arrived at the party by taxi from central London at around seven pm on a bright summer's evening. Hugh was feeling in need for a drink, as it had been a long hot day. A glass of champagne was handed to Hugh as he was saying his hellos and wishing his ex-wife, a very happy birthday.

Suddenly, he was approached by a powerful looking man in his early sixties who kissed Hugh full on the mouth. It was Albert Edwards, a well known international abstract painter whom Hugh had known from when he had lived in Islington in North London, when Hugh had been married to his first wife Giselle. People looked round as Albert kissed Hugh on the mouth. Hugh thought what a pretentious sod, still playing the risqué artist in society role, a man without convention.

'Albert, long time no see, how are you doing,' Hugh piped up.

'Well OK thanks, moved out of London to Herefordshire, gives me more room for my work,' Albert replied stepping closer to Hugh.

Hugh noticed that Albert's breath was same as it always had been, ridden with halitosis.

'Yes we moved out too, some eight years ago to Norfolk. This party of Giselle's has worked out for me as I had to collect a couple of pieces from the Royal Academy Summer Exhibition this afternoon,' said Hugh.

'I did not know you painted, I thought you studied film and television at the Royal College of Art,' cut in Albert.

'I thought I would give it a go. My daughter's turned out to be a very good portrait painter. It was sort of a dry run. I presume you would not enter anything so lowly as the Summer Exhibition, there were over twelve hundred entrants. You usually do a solo at the Tate, don't you?' Hugh said deferentially.

'Actually I had five works in this year's Summer Exhibition, I have just been elected an Academician, you must have seen my works in the Salon two and five, and there was one of my works shown in the brochure too.'

'Oh there were an amazing number of works, maybe I was just not expecting to see your works, we were a bit pushed for time to,' said Hugh trying to cover his tracks.

'Small world Hugh,' said Albert turning away from Hugh.

Next up was Albert's wife Susan who looked somewhat harassed, but had on a smart looking black designer coat.

'Susan, how are you. It's been quite a time since we last met,' asked Hugh.

'Yes, eight years or so, how time flies Hugh.'

'I must say that coat you are wearing looks absolutely fabulous, genuine Cossack feel to it. Is it Russian ?' said Hugh trying to be engaging.

'Actually no Hugh I got this from Joseph's in Knightsbridge,' said Susan frostily.

'I hear Albert had five works in the Summer Exhibition at the Royal Academy,' enquired Hugh.

'That's right he never stops working.'

'Amazing these abstract works of art. I think I will get another drink, you alright for one ?'

'Yes thank you,' said Susan walking away.

Hugh had always had difficulty understanding Albert's abstract paintings, not because he did not appreciate abstract art but he really could not see much in Albert's works. Plus Albert seemed to be somewhat glib about his works, years ago. He had done some very large blank canvas type pictures, one or two colour washes with a blob or two of different colour, twenty feet by twelve feet long. Back in his Islington period.

Apparently these were for an exhibition in New York. Hugh had enquired as to how Albert would ship these huge canvases to New York. Albert said that he would not bother to ship them there, but paint similar ones when he arrived in New York!

To Hugh this made a bit of a mockery of art and all the massively hard work that went into other areas of art such as classical painting and sketches, as in Goya's, Rembrandt's portraits and Leonardo da Vinci's works. But it was just amazing what sold today in the contemporary art market and at what prices, as Hugh's recent studies had revealed.

In fact Hugh and Petra had walked straight past Albert's works at the Summer Exhibition not even seeing who had painted them. It was only afterwards when Hugh looked through the brochure that he realized Albert had been elected as an Academician and that he had five works of art in the Summer Exhibition.

On reflection Hugh thought it must be an awful strain to keep up such a level of pretension as seemed to be reflected in Albert's works. Then he decided that he was probably jealous of Albert, and all his glory and recognition in the art world.

After the party everybody walked down the street to a Thai restaurant. It all seemed so wonderful, so metropolitan, and all on a summer's evening.

There was one long table set out for about some forty people in the restaurant. Hugh tried his hardest to get other people seated around him, so that he would not have to talk to Albert again.

He ordered lots of beer to keep people happy. However, when a couple of guests went to the lavatory, Albert managed to engineer himself back to sitting opposite Hugh.

'Long time since I had a Thai meal, living out in the sticks now, and all that,' said Hugh.

'Really. I used to live out in Thailand for a while, many moons ago, after my student days at the Central. That's where I got some of my ideas from, for those big abstract paintings I did in my Islington days.'

'Oh yes I remember those, the huge canvasses that were shipped to New York.'

'Yes those ones....that's thirty years ago now, some of my finest work I reckon,' said Albert laughing at Hugh.

'More than likely, but what would I know,' replied Hugh looking down into his beer and secretly smiling.

TWELVE GARDENS

(These words were found written in an old exercise book, in a gardener's shed in South Norfolk)

PROLOGUE:

One can philosophize about life till the cows come home, and still not come up with the right answer. A person's life can be seen through their artefacts....

portrait painters' great art, architects' their buildings, politicians their speeches and manifestos, writers their literature, and media people's films and television programmes. The rich and successful, tend to think that they are in a world of their own, whereas bricklayers, house painters and decorators, and gardeners are a forgotten class. Looking round cities or stately homes, it is not only the lasting architecture, the stone and brick work that means so much. It is the gardens too.

Gardens can be an ever evolving seasonal paradise, or they can be a dismal stinking tip. For some, working in the garden can give the feeling of going back to nature and of being close to our primitive ancestors. Fresh air, out of the house, living in the open, working with our hands, that's what's good for us, just like the other half of the Rule of St. Benedict, so the medieval monk said, mental activity in the morning and gardening and other physical activities in the afternoon.

For me it has been a continual horticultural journey, both urban and rural.

FIRST GARDEN

My first memories as a child were in a suburban garden off that long road that runs through North London, the Finchley Road. To me it seemed like a vast expanse of green lawn, shrubs and trees. It was in fact part of the great suburban movement of the

1920's and 1930's. Hampstead Garden Suburb. All the gardens faced each other, with several streets forming a rectangular four or five acre plot of gardens, some bigger than others, all different. On one side in the distance the Northern Line tube train rumbled on, now above ground, rattling slowly onto far distant rustic suburban semi-detached dreams.

In suburbia the fence is the defining moment. Our garden was trussed up on three sides, with creosoted brown fencing planks which I could not see over, but as a child I could look through the cracks, especially where the knot holes had fallen out of the wood fencing.

The house next door, our semi other half, was divided up into two flats. As a very small child I remember this eternal wailing coming from upstairs, then the words,

'I forgive them. I forgive them. I forgive them.'

More wailing, welcome to the Holocaust. They were German refugee Jews, most of whose relatives had been murdered by the Nazis. There they were sitting up there in their flat wailing in the suburbs, with me standing in the garden, looking up at their windows, wondering what was going on. Their name was Mr. and Mrs. Hamburger. In the 1947 the war was still not really over. Death, poverty, destruction and misery were the other side of all the victory celebrations and parades. I was three years old and learning quick.

Everybody supposedly liked gardening in the suburbs. The sound of hand pushed lawn mowers, and hedges being clipped was very much part of my sound effects library of the time. Today, there is one long mechanical grinding noise emanating from gardens, as the latest power driven tool is used to drive all the neighbours crazy.

We had a traditional layout with a rectangular garden lawn surrounded on three sides with flowers beds, and a few smallish trees. At the top of the garden was a concrete patio backing onto the house, with the kitchen door and French doors from the lounge, opening on to it. Contained and self-contained.

My father who was an antiques dealer in the West End of London, was very keen on gardening, always rolling up his sleeves and getting a good sweat up too. My mother who was very elegant and who had been a fashion designer before she met my father, used to grace the garden, and try to have refined tea parties in the summer, at the bottom of the garden. The thing about my parents was that they were like chalk and cheese with some dynamite thrown in. You never quite knew when the volcano was going to erupt.

They also spoke three languages fluently, English, German & French.
My father had emigrated from Sudetenland in Czechoslovakia after the First World, via Paris, New York, Paris again, and then London. Protestant with a German surname.

My mother was born near Baden Baden in Bhul, near Strasbourg. She got one of the last ship crossings to England when the First World War was just about to start. She ended up living in West Hampstead, going to a convent school in Willesden North London, and a Belgian finishing school. Catholic all the way.

If my parents wanted to say something privately to each other, more often than not THEY WOULD SPEAK GERMAN......we had just won the war against the Germans. As kids we were into mock English and German battles, with lots of Spitfire planes shooting down Jerry planes. How come my parents were speaking German and in the garden in suburban London?

My father not only loved his roses, but he also loved his vegetables. A neighbor had a large vegetable garden beyond our fence, but generally people tended to grow shrubs and flowers rather than try to get self-sufficient in the suburbs. But my father always liked a bargain. So he grew his own lettuce and cauliflowers. One day as a four year old, I decided that I would pull a few of these up...seemed like a good idea at the time. Not so.

When my father returned from work it was obvious I was for the high jump. In those days if you broke the rules you got a hiding. Nobody really minds a hiding that much, if they are guilty, providing it is not vicious or sadistic. It is the waiting that is the killer. Time passes very slowly when one is young. I had to go to bed and wait for my punishment for wrecking his small vegetable patch in the garden. It was hot in my little room, and I waited and waited. Now all I can remember is the waiting, plus my mother trying to stop my father giving me a canning. Win some, lose some.

Everybody likes to grow runner beans, my father was no exception. As a young child I used to examine these funny old wooden poles with bits of string on them, then up would crawl these leafy, wavy plants with pinkish flowers and eventually long dangly beans would appear, which I would help pick. The trouble was I think my father let them to grow too long, and they got stringy and tough. I am still very suspicious of runner beans today, as I think they always going to be tough and stringy.

Mowing the lawn always seemed to be an effort, my father would sharpen the lawn-mower blades with a long carborundum stone, spitting on the stone as lubrication as he sharpened the steel blades on the mower. I liked the spitting. Still do it now, if there is any sharpening to be done. And plenty of oil in the moving parts. And off we would go, up & down, up and down, getting the stripes in the lawn.

My uncle who lived round the corner, who was terribly English, had played cricket for Sussex, drank a lot of beer, was an account executive for the Dandy and Beano comics which we kids thought was great, always had better stripes than we did. Must have been watching the groundsman doing the cricket pitch before the matches. Emptying the lawn-mower's bin was the thing, carry it over to the rubbish dump and then back again.

I have three older brothers, none of whom showed much inkling towards gardening, my eldest brother went into the car business and motor racing, and turned our garage into service station. My second brother took to playing rugby, sailing, drinking and girls. My third brother became a total swot, plus turning to religion in a big way, then substituted that for becoming a doctor and a heart specialist. So nobody wanted to mow the lawn.

Being the youngest I seemed to be doing a lot of the chores around the house. By helping my mother I suppose I became aware of the suppression of women at an early age. But one thing I did relish when I was older was mowing the lawn.

We had two miniature French poodles, who used to use the garden as their public loo. I used to clear their mess up, but was not adverse to batting the occasional dog turd over the fence to help my batting along.

When we were young my third brother and I used to pass the long hot summers, either swimming or playing cricket in the garden. I was Len Houghton and he was the great Australian cricketer Don Bradman. If you hit the back fence it was four runs, full toss into it was six, two side fences, runs only.

What games we had, day after day, hour after hour. The poor fences were never the same.

Apart from swotting and playing cricket, my third brother suffered from acidosis, a kind of stomach sickness which seems to have disappeared off the medical map today. It meant that he had to have a lot of fresh eggs.

After the Second World War, there was not much food around, there was government rationing, and hard as it is to believe today, if you wanted extra eggs you had to get your own chickens. I remember these funny looking sheds appearing in the garden, something to do with my father, gerry-built and very slippery inside with all the chicken shit. They were made of asbestos, the MDF of the 1940's & 1950's. There were two of them parked on the left-handside of the garden, next to the bonfire heap. I would stomp down the garden and secretly lift the asbestos flaps over the chicken boxes to see if there were any eggs there. It was all very exciting.

Sometimes the chickens were allowed out to bask in the sun and nestle down in the earth borders, very much changing the ordered feel of the garden.

Like many people in those days we keep pet rabbits on piece of concrete round the back of the garage, which led down to some coal bunkers which backed onto the garden. It was here that I was introduced to the life and death cycle in a big way.

My father used to kill the occasional chicken, usually by hanging it on the knob of the door that led from the garden to the garage. The chicken would flap away there, next to the rabbits, with us kids just staring from the garden. One time I think my father decided to try out the headless chicken theory, with the result that he chopped the chicken's head off, instead of hanging it, and the poor chicken literally ran round the garden headless. More stunning speechless amazement.

If we had a chicken from the garden, for dinner or Sunday lunch it was definitely something of a big treat. Now we gobble them up daily, by the millions without batting an eyelid. I think my father decided that he might start breeding them, so he got a cockerel which he kept in an old incinerator, a good part of the time. This whole process produced much consternation between my mother and father.

My mother who was something of a snob was very much prone to worrying about what the neighbours might think. My father who had emigrated from Sudetenland, Czechoslovakia at the end of the First World War, via Paris and New York, and then to London, did not seem to care that much, mumbling about 'the bourgeoisie' a good deal of the time. Or he would have a quiet swear in German.

The cockerel crowed away early each morning over the start of a long hot summer. The neighbours complained, I mean you could not turn their suburban paradise into a farmyard....what next cows and pigs. My parents bickered about it. I looked at the cockerel crowing in the incinerator and did think that possibly the peace and quiet of the garden had been shattered. It had to go. This is where the headless chicken memory started.

Apart from growing flowers and plants, our garden acted as an important gathering point. My first school was a Catholic Kindergarten school, run by nuns. After being inducted into the Catholic faith, I had made my First Holy Communion, definitely joining the Catholic in-crowd. I had on my new school uniform and I was at one with God. I had this wonderful feeling, like a Vestial virgin. What did I do when I got home, I ran straight into the garden, stood there feeling wonderful and very special, then I had a good go on the swing in the garden.

Years later, my second brother, the rugger bugger, held his wedding reception at our house. At one stage the reception spilled out into the garden. Particularly memorable, was the scene of a human tower, like some circus act, being built up in the garden, with my brother singing at the top of this human pile, made up from his mates at the rugby club.

At the bottom of the garden the neighbours had two boys our age. We had long running battles with them, even resorting to throwing lumps of coal at each other. No real harm done. We also used to use the end of the gardens for joint fireworks displays on Guy Fawkes's Night. This tended to be a little risky, what with jumping jacks and bangers going off all around.

One year I was handed a lit banger which I threw away just in time. The joint firework parties were called off after that.

There was an apple tree at the bottom of the garden which we loved climbing in. It also acted as a way over into another neighbour's garden which had an abandoned feel about it and was all over grown. When the apple tree had fruit on we used to shake the tree to get the cooking apples down for my mother. Collecting them was the big thing. I can almost touch that tree today in my mind, I spent so much time up it. Next to it stood a golden Laburnum tree, with its wonderful dancing, yellow dangly flowers.

As a teenager, I continued to help in the garden, mowing the lawn mostly. In one of the flats next door some young single girls had moved in. When it was hot they used to sunbathe in their garden. I used to say hello. And as they were lying there in their bikinis, I would try to take a quick look through the fence. Just the sort of thing to give a young teenage boy night sweats.

Much of this activity used to happen on Saturday mornings, the garden seemed to have a regular time clock of its own. A rhythm, a pattern. Nine o'clock felt different to eleven o'clock, then afternoon, and at the end of the day children always asking to stay out longer. Apart from the seasons changing, it seems that time is felt more strongly in a garden, than possibly inside a house.

With the seasons passing, time gave a forlorn look to our garden in winter. Often I used to stare out of the window from my little bedroom above the kitchen. Everything seemed to look bare and wretched, waiting for renewal. I could clearly see how our garden was surrounded by other houses too.

Sometimes, I used to think about the sheer power of plants and flowers growing from a small bulbs developing into a daffodil or a wonderful tulip.
A good part of my time was now spent away at boarding school, so whenever I came home I noticed big changes in the garden, as the seasons moved on.

In autumn one year some old cabbages were left to rot in our garden. They looked so bizarre and unreal, with their sagging heads. Years later I saw in art history book, that the Glaswegian painter and designer Charles Renee Macintosh had in one of his lesser moments painted a series of Cabbages in Autumn, perfectly capturing their autumnal decline and decadence.

Like most aspiring middle class children I had to study for long periods of time, especially when I was a teenager, having moved to a Benedictine day school in London. For hours I would be up in my bedroom reading, writing essays, and revising, and then looking out of the window to see what was going on in the garden.

One summer, I had some walnuts that I had been eating. I had cleared away the shells of the eaten ones, I supposedly had finished studying, came downstairs and went into the garden for a rest. Later I came back upstairs and found that some walnuts had been cracked in a different way. This was the arrival of my first jackdaw. I saw him a few times after that.

Then one morning I was sitting up in bed with the window open and in flew the jackdaw and sat on the table next to the bed where my radio was. In a flash he picked up my house keys in his beak and was gone. I leapt out of bed, ran into the garden, shouted at the bird, who dropped the keys at the bottom of the furthest garden fence.

Bird life was rich in the garden, I had made a special bird-box for the blue tits and nailed it up in the old Hawthorn tree. Blue tits are very prolific breeders having at least two batches of eleven or twelve babies. When they first nested, I took the lid off the bird-box, for a quick look, an incredible sight of all these tiny pink fluffy birds with their beaks pointed up for food, all squawking quietly away. It seemed like an awful lot of beaks to feed.

Blackbirds, thrushes, coal tits, robins, chaffinches, sparrows by the dozen, starlings, pigeons, rooks and swallows, house martins and high flying swifts in the summer were part of the regular chorus of bird song and life there.

As the youngest brother I got plenty of hand me downs, including vests, pants, trousers and the odd poke in the ribs. When I was in my last term at school I was handed down my second brother's pre-war Morris 8 car, with running boards, leather seats, and blinds in the rear of the car. But the engine was blown.

As I was planning a European motoring holiday with my school chums, after we had finished our exams and left school finally, I had to get on with re-conditioning the car engine. Once I had got the engine out, I decided that the best place to lay all the parts out was in one corner of the garden. The car had side valves which all had to be ground in properly. The action is rather like trying to make fire by rubbing a stick between your fingers.

My elder brothers used to advise me on how I should or should not do repairs to the engine. Eventually, I got it all back together again, gaskets and all. The garden needed a good clean up. My father seemed amused by it all, but my mother looked on in disbelief.

My mother used to hang washing out on a line that went across the width of the garden. If you wanted to cross the patio from the kitchen, to get coal or coke in, or just run round the garden, you often had to fight the washing. But the washing would always come down if we had guests round.

And we seemed to have had plenty of those, especially the Catholic priests from our local church down the road. It was either Sherry or tea or both and in the summer more often than not taken in the garden. As a small boy I remember the hand of God's disciple on earth handing me an empty Sherry glass for a quick re-fill, before returning to his priestly duties in the sacristy at the church.

The deck chairs were much in evidence in the garden. My father loved to sunbathe and doze off in one. Guests were often given one. One of my father's friends who seemed to fancy my mother, sat in one that collapsed, which everybody thought was very funny.

We would have tea and sandwiches in the garden, but very rarely eat a full meal outside. I think people were stricter then about eating your meals at the dreaded table.

My mother used to have many guests over who often had something to do with the Catholic church, as she belonged to the Legion of Mary. It was a sort of missionary organization for good works, in the suburbs and beyond. Charity and good works.

My mother got involved with helping out Thalidomide children, many of whom did not have properly formed arms and legs, as a result of their mothers having been prescribed the Thalidomide drug during pregnancy. So much so that she held a garden party for these mal-formed children.
I was asked to help out.

I can remember our garden full of these wonderful brave children, stumbling around, but having fun. There was one little brave boy with no proper arms, who struggled up the kitchen step from the garden. A poignant moment for me. My father did not approve of all this, so these children never came to our garden again.

My parents seemed to entertain quite a bit, having cocktail parties for their friends, mainly local neighbours. I often found these parties tedious, but had to help handing round the sausages and bridge rolls, and asking people if they wanted another drink, which they always seemed to want.

I think I must have come down for the vacation, from my provincial university, when they had another of these cocktail parties which I thought was extremely tedious and full of hypocrites. As we had net curtains over the doors into the garden, nobody saw me peeing against the doors, in my anti bourgeois fury and bohemian stance!

Things got worse as I got older and I possibly thought I could be more irresponsible, mostly by getting drunk and reading existentialist books, which depressed the hell out of me.

But it was always to the garden that I returned. I remember one occasion when I had had a session with some friends in Oxford, whilst wearing an old army greatcoat, had got home in a bit of a state, and decided that the best place to sleep it off, was in a deckchair in the garden. It was the tag end of winter.

This habit expanded, and I can remember waking up in Kensington Gardens one summer morning wondering how I got there, having slept in a deckchair next to the Albert Memorial. It is not that hard to become a street person.

When I was at university, I was possibly suffering from garden deprivation. So I got into wondering around grave yards, plus listening to church organ music and reading ghost stories, but my daily contact with gardens was zero, looking out of bedsits or college rooms.

My nearest thing to a garden was a window ledge on which I used to cool my home-made packet cream caramel puddings, plus feeding the odd mangy pigeon.

My father, who knew his limits in terms of gardening, used to love a good gardening session after Church on Sunday mornings, mainly in the front garden of our big semi-detached house in North London.

He loved his roses. He worked at it and used to get up a sweat. My mother, after our Sunday breakfast would also be working up a sweat, getting the Sunday roast on. Eventually the two would meet over lunch and the sparks would fly.

I might mow the back lawn and then help my mother in the kitchen, which was definitely like working in a hot hotel kitchen. The kitchen door to the garden was more often than not open. It had two cracked wooden steps down to the patio.

My mother never gardened, but she loved gardens for the peace and serenity that they seemed to give her. As a Catholic my mother would often go on retreat for peace and quiet, and contemplation to a large country house with lovely gardens to walk and reflect in.

One of the last things my father did for the garden was to plant some little apple trees in one of the borders. I can remember the concentrated blossom and the small apples they produced. After he had his stroke, and stopped working at seventy eight, he used to sit in the drawing room as my mother called it, and spend some of his day looking out at the garden, as well as asking for 'mountain fresh' tap water.

So my first real garden become rather sad and uncared for. I had left home many moons ago. All those cricket games, lawn mowing, tree climbing, summer afternoons and my mother's tea parties, my father snoozing in his deck chair in the sun, accepting what was there, me looking over the fence....they were all long gone.

SECOND GARDEN

I left home pretty early, first to go north to university and then I got married and ended up in Wymondham in South Norfolk.

My first job was as a teacher in a school that reminded me very much of the one described by Evelyn Waugh in 'Decline and Fall', with a pompous head master, wild and eccentric teaching staff, and pupils who had an examination failure rate second to none.

I rented a little first floor flat in the old town centre of Wymondham, in a Queen Anne house, which had an abandoned garden. I could feel the history there, with its decaying plants and shrubs, plus pieces of broken pottery from large flower pots, discarded over the centuries. The garden had a very peaceful feel about it. Sometimes, I used to walk round it with my new wife. It felt as if we were in a suspended time zone.

The school itself was a few miles away, and the annual parents day was when the boys really learnt how to garden and do house maintenance. Instead of preparing for examinations most of them were dragooned into getting the buildings and gardens up to scratch for the parents 'Open Day,' a dull imitation of the Etonian summer party.

This rustic extravaganza was off-set by my going back to my little flat, where my wife had made a nice home, cooked good meals, and seemed to read all day. Maybe it was because I did not have a real garden that I became restless.

Mind you I was young and wanted to become a poet at the time. Possibly I thought I had to be Bohemian and wild. I would shuffle round the old back yard and pick the odd flower or weed in the garden and have a 'moody'.

On my days off, I would go to Norwich Library and read novels and poetry. I can remember staring out the window as the rain poured down, thinking 'is this it?'....married, teaching and earning the grand sum of £54 per month after tax.

Well it wasn't. We went back to London and I did a post-graduate degree in something that I thought was very meaningful, involving Literature, Sociology and Film Studies. We ended up in a first floor flat in the Upper Richmond Road, with no garden but with a very big park to walk round. Richmond Park even had wild deer, so it must have been good.

Not long after, when I was tutoring part-time A Level students in Economics, Sociology and Politics, there was a Ghanian student who I quite liked. He asked me round for a breakfast and to meet his wife. We had grilled fish and drank sherry. As it was very hot in his small flat near Wormwood Scrubs, one of London's largest prisons, I suggested that we went to Richmond Park as I did not have a garden.

Whilst walking in the Savannah like long grass , in Richmond Park, he said that this part of the park reminded him of Africa and Ghana. Wild deers rustled through the grass and I thought who needs a garden when you have got this.

As a child I had grown up fully using Hampstead Heath, from walks with my mother to charging around on our bikes to tobogganing down the slopes when it snowed.

For a child, and even now these wonderful laid out parks, partly wild, partly formalised represent a kind of open garden for me. They are an essential breathing spaces, as city life hammers away at those green doors.

THIRD GARDEN

Inevitably the pressures of living in a small rented flat meant that my wife and I looked for a small house with a garden. Guess what...just down the road from her parents in Datchet, lies Windsor in all its Royal and military glory. The house seemed affordable at £7,500, and my Dad was going to help me with the deposit.

But things had not been going too well with my wife and I. She never seemed to be able to forget about any small misdemeanour on my behalf, like having too much beer. OK, a telling off, an earful and that is it, but not next week and then the week after as well.

There was temptation too for me. My wife used to teach drama with her BBC drama director brother who was RADA trained, in Datchet, Windsor every Saturday, all day. I had the whole day to myself, plus my mates round the corner.

At a New Year's Eve party near Welshpool, in Wales which my wife refused to go to as she did not like my lawyer friend from university, who had invited us, I met this stunning woman. Separation loomed, my daughter was less than a year old.

One day I packed them off to their grand-mother. I stayed in the flat, then fled to Greenwich and finally ended up with the house and a garden in Windsor with the new love of my life.

Frances Road in Windsor was another suburban road, surrounded by quiet streets. The gardens were quite long and had been developed up over the years. The house need completely doing up as did the garden. My mate Peter, from Ealing in West London, came down.

We turned on the electricity and the mains water and then went to the pub up the road.

We came back to find the water pipe had fractured, leaking water all over the kitchen ceiling which had partially collapsed as a result, with water everywhere.

So the garden started to get filled up with building junk.

Plus we used to drink and eat out there. I can remember the garden being a little dark at the top end away from the house.

There was also an access point from the lane behind and...

(These stories to be continued.... some film, some urban, some rustic, and also about those other nine gardens.)

THE END

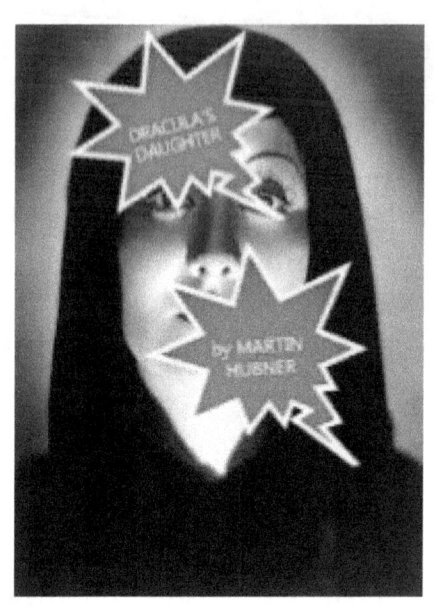

www.ingramcontent.com/pod-product-compliance
Lightning Source LLC
Chambersburg PA
CBHW050205230526
45470CB00001B/252